MARTIAL'S EPIGRAMS

TRANSLATIONS AND IMITATIONS

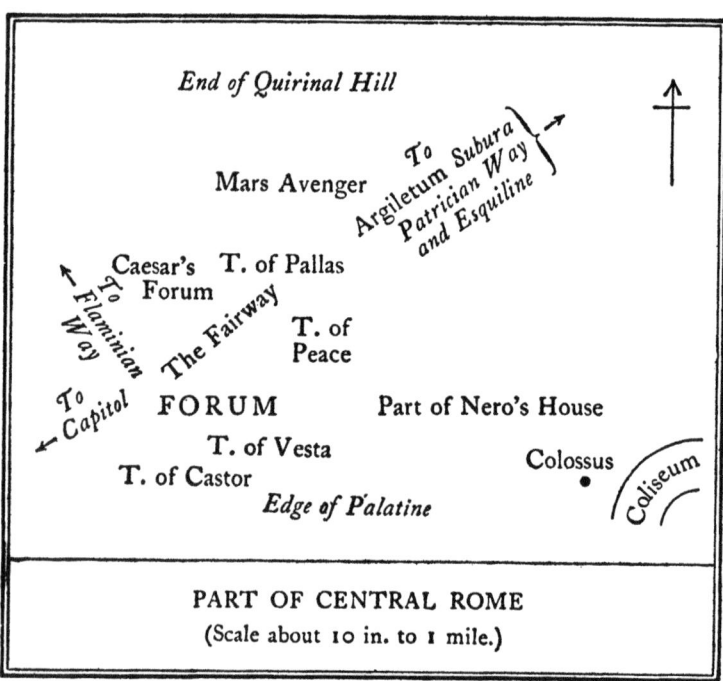

PART OF CENTRAL ROME
(Scale about 10 in. to 1 mile.)

MARTIAL'S EPIGRAMS

TRANSLATIONS AND IMITATIONS

BY

A. L. FRANCIS, M.A.

*Sometime Fellow of Jesus College, Cambridge, and late Head Master
of Blundell's School, Tiverton*

AND

H. F. TATUM, M.A.

*Sometime Scholar of Balliol College, Oxford, and Ireland University
Scholar, late Assistant Master of Blundell's School, Tiverton*

CAMBRIDGE

AT THE UNIVERSITY PRESS

1924

CAMBRIDGE
UNIVERSITY PRESS

University Printing House, Cambridge CB2 8BS, United Kingdom

Published in the United States of America by Cambridge University Press, New York

Cambridge University Press is part of the University of Cambridge.

It furthers the University's mission by disseminating knowledge in the pursuit of education, learning and research at the highest international levels of excellence.

www.cambridge.org
Information on this title: www.cambridge.org/9781107695153

First published 1924
First paperback edition 2014

A catalogue record for this publication is available from the British Library

ISBN 978-1-107-69515-3 Paperback

PREFACE

MARTIAL stands alone in his age as the poet of friendship, private life and simple emotions. Modest, simple and affectionate, he is as much at home in idyll or elegy as in epigram; the latter in a sarcastic sense is rare with him. For his flattery of patrons we may blame his want of spirit but shall not question his sincerity. He saw no doubt the best side of their characters. His eulogies of Regulus or Sulpicia may be exaggerated but have a truer ring than the studied phrases of the *Agricola*.

Literature as a political force had died with Augustus. Lucan's attempt to revive it was grotesque, and Tacitus and Juvenal had not yet come. Martial himself is no republican, and (like Thackeray) accepts society as he finds it. With his tongue in his cheek he calls Domitian the "mighty Thunderer" and accepts provisionally that craze of his about Hercules which reads so curiously now, as well as society phrases like *rex et dominus, dominus et deus noster* (not *meus*) applied to human beings. This matter will be more fully considered below.

Some modernisms in the translations perhaps need apology. They have, we may say, Dryden's authority. A phrase of Shakespeare, a sporting allusion, or a proper name unknown to the classics may be pardoned if in the spirit of the original. Once or twice a frank imitation has crept in where it had no business, but these are few and are easily skipped.

The numbers are those of Paley's Edition.

A. L. F.
H. F. T.

ACCOUNT OF THE AUTHOR

THERE is little known about the life of Martial except that he was born at Bilbilis in Spain, and was thus a compatriot of Seneca, Juvenal and Lucan, that he wrote in Rome during the reigns of Titus, Domitian, Nerva and Trajan, and that he returned to Spain three years after the death of Domitian and ended his life there on an estate given him by a certain Marcella, perhaps his second wife. At Rome he had the rank of a knight as well as other privileges properly bestowed on men with families*.

The first nine books of the epigrams were published under Domitian (the first after the second as is seen by the first epigram of either book), the tenth under Nerva, the two final books succeeded a period of idleness and were written under Trajan, the last in Spain.

Tacitus is very unkind in the opening of the *Agricola* where he alludes to the literary silence of the fifteen years of Domitian. Neither he nor Juvenal wrote during that time, but Martial was writing all the while. Perhaps neither read the other's works. On the other hand Pliny the Younger, who is by no means a flatterer, admires him as *homo ingeniosus acutus acer* and especially mentions his *candor*—a word implying what has been called "faithful dealing"—together with a kind heart†.

The friendship was reciprocal as may be seen from Ep. 522; what may be blamed in Martial is that he is too indiscriminate, for instance in his compliments not only to the emperor but to such informers as the "good" Regulus. This sanctimonious impostor is well exposed by Pliny who disliked him‡, but Martial's attitude is not without parallels. The case of Domitian

* Ep. 108.   † Ep. 3, 31.   ‡ Ep. 4, 2, 7.

is more flagrant; the flattery is "gross, open, palpable," but for that very reason it differs essentially from the underhand and malignant flattery associated with tyrants and their victims. Lucan went much further and was less sincere; *i.e.* he hated in his heart that which he praised. But a great deal of this nonsense about the emperor's divinity etc. was conventional. When Domitian changed the head of Hercules for his own nobody laughed at him, and so the allusion could be made with no more shame than saying "your grace" to a duke, indeed it would be expected, to refuse would be not only unsafe but rude. And silence was no alternative. Every now and then the question arose as to whether death was better. Martial approves of Decianus' choice (Ep. 5)—to "live and live unblamed," like the Matius of Caesar's day rather than the Brutus. And so he allows himself most high-flown language about "Hercules the Greater," without malice certainly, and one may hope with a little disgust. More displeasing perhaps are the compliments paid to Domitian's military successes, which were not unmixed. It is curious that Martial had failed to recognize Domitian's really valuable work (Bury) on the Taunus boundary (Ep. 3).

The temptation to over-politeness in an author is difficult to realize for us to whom even "gentle reader" is out of date. Books were no dearer then than they are now, and readers beyond comparison fewer, so that it was impossible for an author to support himself. If a poor man, he must become the client of a "patron."

This meant, besides a strained vocabulary, a wearisome attendance sometimes lasting all day, but at least beginning with a call in the early morning in the white toga, in all weathers and at any distance. Each patron had many clients and *vice versâ*. Great assiduity might secure an invitation to dinner, but the usual substitute was a "dole" of 25 ases or about half a crown. The abuses which followed when the patron was ill-bred form a stock subject of Martial and Juvenal; that Martial himself gradually won a better position may be partly gathered from expressions in later books; *e.g.* his farm at Nomentum is "a barren waste" in Ep. 83, but in Ep. 297 is "a suburban snug recess," unless indeed the latter is a new acquisition, which amounts to the same thing; or even from his language in accepting the tiny present of Ep. 601, which, whatever it might have been, was probably worth having. A description of his engagements in Ep. 561 does not include morning attendance on patrons, although he has to call for his "dole" still at dinner time.

The worst excesses of flattery came to an end with the death of Domitian. Martial is glad of the relief, but in the epigram (563) "In vain you stand, soft Flattery" there is no unkind feeling expressed to the dead, only satisfaction at freedom from the strain of courtly language. But he was tired of a life of dependence, and the gift of an estate in Spain by Marcella led to his permanent withdrawal to that country.

MARTIAL'S EPIGRAMS

*The numbers are those of Paley's Selection,
one or two being omitted*

1 (I. ii)

ON A BOUND COPY OF HIS WORK

Reader, if you with book of mine would share
A tedious journey and a foreign air,
'Tis yours; a wider fits your archives' space,
Me dainty vellum and a hand's embrace.
Where am I sold? You shall not wander wide
Through the whole town; a hint will be your guide.
By Pallas Fair-Way and the Goddess meek*
Leucensis' literary hostel seek.

* The Forum of Pallas and the Temple of Peace.

2 (I. iii)

For Argiletum's* crowded shelves you pine;
Fie, little book, there's room enough in mine.
Alas, you know not Rome's fastidious frown;
It's far too critical, our ancient town;
From old and young contemptuous grunts arising
Suggest rhinoceros ventriloquizing;
You'll toss your kisses to the loud bravo,
Then in a blanket to the zenith go.
What? if I choose to change a few expressions
And pour cold water on some indiscretions,
The rascal must have wings and fly away!
Off with you! but 'twere safer far to stay.

* Between the Forum and the Suburra or business quarter.

3 (I. iv)

TO DOMITIAN

Caesar, if e'er these verses reach your ear,
Put off the frown that bows the world in fear.
Your lays have been a target for my fun
And I have chaffed the triumphs you have won;
But with that kindly aspect read my rhyme
With which you watch fair Thymele* or the mime.
Your censure well such license may endure;
My page is wanton, but my life is pure.

* An actress.

4 (I. v)

DOMITIAN TO THE AUTHOR

(The sea-fight was an exhibition on prepared water.)

For epigram-floating a chance
  My sea-fight will help you to get;
But, Marcus, be warned in advance,
  Such "floating" your bark may upset!

5 (I. viii)

Wise Cato you admire and Thrasea* great,
Embrace their principles but not their fate,
Nor with bare breast defy resistless force.
Well, Decianus, I your choice endorse;
I want no hero by his dying famed,
Him rather who can live and live unblamed.

* An opponent and victim of Nero.

6 (I. ix)

A LEGACY WOOER

For Maronilla's hand Gemellus sues,
With prayers and gifts and yearning sighs he woos.
Is she so fair then? Hideous, heaven forgive her!
What subtler charm then moves his heart? Her liver.

7 (I. xi)

A Knight's allowed ten sesterces*, you drink
Two millions worth, Sextilian, I should think.
Hot water flagons soon had failed, but you're
Content with wine, Sextilianus, pure.

* For refreshment at the public shows, compare Ep. 219.

8 (I. xii)

By cool Alcides' height you take your way,
Where Tibur steams with sulphur waters grey.
By rural wood and minstrel-haunted down,
A rustic stone marks the fourth mile from town.
A rough-built cloister gave a summer shade—
Ah, cloister, from what brink of murder stayed!
For scarce had godly Regulus* driven by,
Behold in ruins the vast fabric lie.
Fortune no doubt, at our just plaints concerned,
For very shame the threatening blow had turned.
Now welcome, loss, and danger! Had they missed
These arches, who would know that gods exist?

* The pleader of Ep. 100.

9 (I. xiii)

When faithful Arria handed on the sword,
Red with her life-blood, to her loving lord*,
"Believe me, dear," she said, "I feel no smart;
'Tis but the wound you'll deal that breaks my heart."

* Thrasea Paetus, a victim of Nero; Ep. 5.

10 (I. xv)

Julius, of all my friends the most unfailing,
If faith and hoary trust are aught availing,
Nigh sixty winters do besiege your brow
Yet few the days that you have lived till now;
Delay's the danger; think of time and tide;
'Tis ill postponing what may be denied.
Cares dog the path and sorrow drags her chain,
And but a moment truant joys remain.
Tighten your grasp, and cling with all your might,
Even so they fleet and vanish into night.
"I'll live to-morrow," no wise man will say;
To-morrow is too late. Then live to-day.

11 (I. xvii)

Titus would have me plead. "Your fortune's made;
A tip-top business." So's a farmer's trade.

12 (I. xviii)

What ails you, Tucca, old Falernian red
With deadly flask of Vatican to wed?
What has that filthy liquor done for you?
To this great wine what cruel scaith is due?

Don't think of us. To kill Falernian's sin,—
And carry poison to a heavenly bin.
We guests may possibly deserve our fate,
But such a vintage claims immortal date.

13 (I. xx)

Host, forgetful of your guest
Munching mushrooms of the best,
There in solitary state
While the crowd expectant wait;
Greedy, guzzling glutton, oh!
Hear my prayer before you go.
Be there on your platter seen
*Champignon sauce Agrippine**.

* Agrippina poisoned Claudius with a mushroom.

14 (I. xxv)

Faustinus, give your poems to the nation,
Verses well worthy of your inspiration,
Such as Pandion's* kinsfolk might acclaim
Nor Roman elders by their silence blame.
Fame stands before your threshold, let her in;
Are you ashamed your meed of praise to win?
Your books will long outlive you in their fame;
Come then, begin, for ashes have no name.

* An old king of Athens.

15 (I. xxvi)
For the subject compare Ep. 7.

Five* tiers of tipplers cannot match your greed;
A tank, Sextilian, is what you need.

* Rows of seats in the amphitheatre.

You rob your next-door neighbours of their whole,
Then to the back rows hold your begging bowl *.
This vintage gushed not in Pelignian field
Nor did the Tuscan slope such nectar yield.
You drain a jar of old Opimian wine,
A Marsic cellar did this cask enshrine.
A Laletanian † brand will suit your thirst
If you drink off a million at a burst.

* For wine-tickets.
† A poor wine district in Spain.

16 (I. xxvii)

After ten cups were put away
I said, "Procillus," yesterday,
"You'll dine with me, my friend, you're wanted."
You promptly took the thing for granted
And made a note without formality
Of my incautious hospitality;
A dangerous precedent to set;
I hate a guest who won't forget.

17 (I. xxx)

Diaulus, surgeon, undertaker now,
Still trims a death-bed, as he well knows how.

18 (I. xxxii)

Gellia, alone, ne'er weeps her sire at all;
In company the bidden tears down fall.
True grief is not for admiration shown.
He only weeps indeed, who weeps alone.

19 (I. xxxvi)

Tullus and Lucan, if to you were given
The fate that Leda's sons* once found in heaven,
Between the pair there were this noble strife
Which for his brother should lay down his life.
He'ld say, who first should reach the shore divine,
"Live in your portion, brother, live in mine."

* Pollux gave up half his life for Castor.

20 (I. xl)

Sour critic, who can here no merit find,
May you, unenvied, envy all mankind!

21 (I. xli)

You think yourself a vastly witty knave;
Believe me, you are not. What then? A slave,
Street hawker from beyond the Tiber, bearing
Pale sulphur sticks for vases past repairing,
Or who the peevish adder captive leads
Or merry-making crowd on pea-soup feeds,
Or bawling cook, who from his greasy kitchen
Cheapens the smoking sausages he's rich in;
Or market-drudge who cries salt-fish for master;
Town poet? No, but local poetaster,
Or shameless owner of a Spanish stew;
Cease then to think what none believes but you.
True wit's a gift. Yes, Gabba* though you try
And Tettius Caballus* to outvie.
The man who bawls with brute garrulity
Is not a Tettius, a Caballus† he.

* Comedians.   † A hack.

22 (I. xlii)

When loyal Portia heard her Brutus' fate,
At means of death withdrawn disconsolate,
"Know you not yet death will not be denied?
My father* might have taught you that," she cried,
And gulped the glowing ash. Your pains you lose
When you the dagger, cruel friends, refuse.

* The younger Cato.

23 (I. xliii)

We were guests, we were twenty, we entered your door,
And yesterday nothing was served us but boar.
No lingering grapes were preserved from your home
Nor sweet honey-apples that vie with the comb,
Nor pears that on pleats of genista repose
Nor pomegranates that rival the fugitive rose.
No pillar of Sassina cheese did we find,
Or olives in jar of Picenum enshrined;
'Twas boar, nothing more, and a squeaker, a brat,
No match for a dwarf, an unarmed one at that.
And none for us either. We stared in a row,
And thought we were watching a boar at a show.
May you never have boar for your greediness spread,
But fatten a boar like the slave-boy* instead.

* Perhaps a victim in the amphitheatre.

24 (I. xlv)

For fear my fount of poetry run dry
"Him answering"* is still my cuckoo-cry.

* A tag of Homer.

25 (I. xlix)

Friend, to be sung by Spaniards, and again,
The pride and glory of our native Spain,
Sicilianus, you'll behold, I wis,
Famed for her arms and steeds, your Bilbilis,
Her broken crags, and Gaius hoar with snow
And hallowed peaks of steep Vadavero,
And you will see Boterdus' sacred groves
Rich with the harvest which Pomona loves.
You'll float on Congedus' slow tepid wave
Where the soft Naiads love their limbs to lave.
Your enervated body braced you'll feel
In shallow Salo, lord of tempered steel.
And, while you feast, Voberca's covert near
Will offer to your hand its fallow deer.
By golden Tagus you'll exclude the heat
Deep in the shadow of some cool retreat,
With fresh Dercenna eager thirst dispelling
And Nutha, in mid summer snow excelling.
When hoar December, fierce with wintry blast,
Howls like a madman at my window fast,
You Tarragona's sunny coast will view
And Laletania her charm renew,
And there the gentle deer you will ensnare
And bring to bay the home-bred boar and hare,
A veteran hunter on stout thoroughbred,
While to your bailiff falls the antlered head.
The neighbouring wood will feed a cheerful blaze
Round which a group of rustic children plays.
The huntsman too of welcome will not fail,
A ready guest within an easy hail.

No senatorial shoe, no toga nigh,
No raiment reeking with rich purple dye;
No henchman rude, no client's querulous lay,
Her ladyship's caprices far away;
No wan-faced prisoner* will your dreams affright,
But you will soundly sleep the livelong night.
Let others earn the loud inane bravo;
They are not happy though men style them so.
There you will humbly bask in sunny days,
While Sura's† pleading wins but empty praise.
When honour's debt is paid, there is no shame
Life's paltry balance for one's own to claim.

* A client whom he must defend.
† Perhaps the advocate who caused his banishment.

26 (i. i)

Your "dresser" as Mistyllus is addressed;
Mine shall be Taratalla "all the rest."*

* A parody on the Homeric line.

27 (i. lii)

Here, Quintianus, is my book of verse,
Mine, though these lines I hear your friend rehearse.
If they complain of such a grievous thrall,
Stand up and claim them, and give bail and all.
And then, if he their master claims to be,
Say they are mine and I have set them free.
If thrice and four times this demand you shout
You'll put the shameless book-thief to the rout.

28 (I. liii)

> Yes—you stole and sold my verses—yet within the budget
>   left
> Stands a page—your own all over—to convict you of the
>   theft.
> 'Midst your plunder, what a blunder! such amid the
>   choicest gleam
> Shot from costly Tyrian purple Gallia's coarsest fleece
>   might seem.
> So Arretian ware by contrast flouts the sparkling crystal, so
> Mingled with the swans of Leda by Cayster strays a
>   crow,
> So, when hallowed glades are burning to the Attic warbler's
>   sigh,
> Jarring with her strain of sorrow screams a vile, intrusive
>   pie!
> Now, I ask no proof of title, need no judge to grant relief;
> See, your own dull page confronts you, saying plainly,
>   "You're a thief!"

29 (I. lv)

> Pray would you know what Martial wishes for,
> Fronto, famed ornament of peace and war?
> A simple farm without extravagance,
> And homespun ease in humble circumstance.
> Who would endure the chill of marble halls
> And daily platitude of morning calls,
> When he can reap the spoils of wood and moor
> And spread the wily noose before his door?
> Draw forth the quivering troutlet with a hair,
> Nor the red jar of golden honey spare,

What time the farm-wife loads the tottering board
And home-grown embers roasted eggs afford?
Who loves me not, may he, I humbly ask,
White-clad* and wan pursue his daily task.

* In the official toga.

30 (I. lix)

DOLE VERSUS DINNER

See Ep. 114.

The dole of Baiae yields me pennies twenty
And five*; starvation in the midst of plenty.
Oh! give me back the gloomy baths of yore.
Why bathe in luxury and sup no more?

* 25 ases, say 2s. 6d. A dinner alone would cost more at Baiae.

31 (I. lxi)

Verona loves Catullus,
    To Virgil Mantua's true,
Patavium boasts her Livy,
    Flaccus* and Stella too,
Wet Nile Apollodorus,
    Pelignia Naso's name,
Two Senecas and a Lucan
    Make learned Cordova's fame.
Sing, Merida, Decianus,
    And Canius, Gades dear,
Our names, Licinianus,
    Proud Bilbilis shall hear.

* The poet of Ep. 37. The rest are mostly Martial's friends.

32 (I. lxvi)

To be a poet cheaply do not think;
Applause is more than paper, pen and ink.
Rough drafts, unpublished poems you should steal,
Known to one man and fast with lock and seal,
Watched by the parent of the virgin sheet,
Not soiled with greetings in the crowded street.
A well-known book cannot change authors thus;
It should be something less conspicuous.
I've some that neither boss nor binding show;
Buy them and welcome; not a soul will know.
Who other's work for his would advertise
Must purchase silence with the book he buys.

33 (I. lxix)

Tarentos* used to boast her laughing Pan,
Now she has Canius for her merry man.

* A place in the Campus Martius.

34 (I. lxx)

Go, little book, and pay my morning call
Polite at Proculus' majestic hall.
This is the way, by Castor, shield of Rome,
And hoary Vesta's holy virgin home,
To high Palatium, decked with many a shrine
And many an image of our lord divine.
Nor pause to wonder where with starry crown
Colossus upon him of Rhodes looks down.
Round on the left a mansion you will see
Whose lofty portals claim your courtesy.

There enter, nor expect the frown of pride;
No hospitable gate was e'er so wide,
So dear to Phoebus and the learned Nine.
He'll want the author, not the valentine.
Then tell him, as a poet I'm not vain,
But you're no product of a courtier's brain.

35 (I. lxxi)

Seven ladles for Justina
    And for fair Laevia six,
For Lycas, Lyde, Ida,
    Five, four and three we mix.
Let every love be numbered
    With old Falernian red;
No mistress answers to my call,
    Then come thou, Sleep, instead.

36 (I. lxxii)

Filching my verse, you steal a poet's name
And of a minstrel you would have the fame.
So toothful truthful Aegle claims to be
With purchased bones of Indian ivory;
So fair Lycoris to herself appears
When lead her mulberry complexion clears.
If in this way a poet you'ld be called,
Then, Fidentinus, you'll have locks when bald.

37 (I. lxxvi)

LAW A BETTER PROFESSION THAN POETRY
To Flaccus the poet of Ep. 31.

O precious prize and crown of all my care,
Patavium's hope and foster-son and heir,
Put off your songs and lyric minstrelsy;
No maid of all the Nine will pay your fee.
Phoebus is nought, Minerva owns the chest,
She's wise and she can buy up all the rest
What boots the barren ivy *? Pallas' tree
Bows with dark load its leaves' variety.
Poor Helicon has only brooks and bays
And song's delight and unsubstantial praise.
No more of Cirrha and Permessis drear†;
The Roman mart is richer and more near.
There money rattles, but the author's prize,
Cold salutation, with the echo dies.

* This stood for poetry, the olive for learning.
† Places sacred to Apollo and the Muses.

38 (I. lxxviii)

Festus, poor victim of a foul decay,
When the fell venom claimed his face a prey,
Fond tears reproving and alone dry-eyed,
Determined so to pass the Stygian tide.
No poisoned cup those lips might desecrate,
No lingering famine sealed his tragic fate.
A Roman life he crowned by Roman death
And by a nobler path he shed his breath.
This fate is grander than great Cato's end
And golden-lettered; he was Caesar's friend.

39 (I. lxxix)

You still will be driving, a jury, a trade,
Or something or nothing, mule, donkey or jade;
Drive on, sir, drive on; to keep business alive,
Better drive your own hearse than have nothing to drive.

40 (I. lxxxi)

The aged Canus, failing fast,
Sued for the dole, his first and last.
His need supplied, of grief he died,
At having missed it in the past.

41 (I. lxxxii)

Yon cloister, that with havoc all around
Fell late a dusty ruin to the ground,
In its catastrophe no voice can blame.
For recreation to those arches came
Just Regulus*, and passed, when close behind
The ponderous fabric to its base inclined
And, when its lord had into safety turned,
Lay prostrate, innocent and unconcerned.
Relieved, new comfort in the gods we take,
Who made destruction harmless for your sake.

* See Ep. 100.

42 (I. lxxxv)

When the glib auctioneer was marking down
Bids for an "Eligible site" near town,
"Absurd," he said, "for any to suppose
Marius must sell; he rather lends than owes."

What ails the fellow? "Man and beast and crop
He lost there, so he's not inclined to stop."
Who willingly would bid to lose his all?
We never heard the poisonous hammer fall.

43 (I. lxxxvi)

I've Novius for a neighbour; by the window as I stand
(Oh! you lucky, lucky fellow!) I can touch him with my
    hand.
(He's such a jolly sportsman.) Well, he's really far away
As the governor of Egypt or Syene's chief to-day.
And, not to speak of dinner, I can't see the chap or hear;
There's not a man in all the town so far and yet so near.
So he must shift or I must shift; his tenement or street
Let others share, who do not care, like me, his face to
    meet.

44 (I. lxxxviii)

Reft from thy lord, dear lad, in budding spring,
Beneath Labicum's turf now slumbering,
No idle bulk of Parian architrave
With toil ephemeral shall mark thy grave,
But docile box and mantling shoots of vine
With meadows watered by these tears of mine.
Take then, dear child, these tokens of my sorrow;
Here shall thy name dwell through the long to-morrow.
And when the fates have spun mine utmost thread
Here would thy master share thy lowly bed.

45 (I. lxxxix)

Cinna, you whisper still in every ear
Nonsense and secrets which the world might hear,
Laugh in a whisper, moan and weep and blame,
Sing and pass sentence, hold your peace, declaim;
And, so deepseated is this voice disease,
You even whisper Caesar's eulogies.

46 (I. xciii)

Fabricius lies here, Aquinus nigh,
Proud first to wing his journey to the sky.
Two altars to record their service rise,
But greater honour these brief words comprise:
"One record theirs of faithful service done,
But, greater miracle, their hearts were one."

47 (I. xcvii)

You think yourself a mighty clever fellow,
    Because mid crowds and din you speak with ease.
To plead is not to bleat while others bellow.
    Silence in court there! Now sir, if you please!

48 (I. xcix)

You had scarcely two millions, but made such display,
Were so lavish, Calenus, in giving away,
That we wished you ten million. Good fortune was kind
And kept our devout aspiration in mind.
Seven months and four deaths brought our wishes to pass,
Had you used them to any account! But, alas!

As if you'd been robbed of ten million at least,
You turned niggard and miser. Your sumptuous feast,
Such as once in a twelve-month your thrift can afford,
A few dirty coppers displayed on your board.
For seven aged cronies, your table around,
Your banqueting cost you a leaden half-pound*.
What prayer shall we offer to meet your desert?
With ten times the fortune you'll starve for a cert.

* *I.e.*, of adulterated silver.

49 (I. c)

Of "mas" and "dadas" she may lisp; I'll wager,
Compared to them, she's much the older stager.

50 (I. ci)

Demetrius, of penmen shrewdest, best,
Known to our sovereign, to his master blest,
Too soon cut off, has perished in his prime,
Four years, three lustres his allotted time.
But, that he might not pass the Stygian wave,
Seared by the fatal malady, a slave,
I gave him liberty; had he his due
I would have freed him from his sickness too.
He felt the boon and with a freeman's breath
He hailed me "Patron"* on the brink of death.

* A liberated slave became the client of his master.

51 (I. cii)

Dressed out in your smartest
You sat to the artist
For a portrait of Venus,
    Lycoris the vain;

But wishing to serve a
Good turn to Minerva,
He painted her rival
    Confoundedly plain.

52 (I. ciii)

"Would the kind gods a million* offer me,"
Scaevola, you said, ere yet of knight's degree,
"How rich, how bounteous would be my lot!"
The gods were generous, but you forgot.
Your toga fouler grew and cloak together,
Your shoe was patched three times and four with leather.
Of some ten olives nine were put away,
And dinner laid but every other day,
Your red Veientine's rough with native earth,
Mistress and porridge make three pennyworth.
I'll go to law; swindler, defaulter black!
Or live, or give the gods their million back.

* £8000 which would entitle him to the rank of senator.

53 (I. civ)

If speckled pards the dainty yoke obey
And savage lions own the trainer's sway,
If antlered monarchs champ the golden bit,
And bears of Libya to the yoke submit,
If boars like him of Calydonian* brake
Direction from their purple halter take,
If ugly bisons gay in harness go
And elephants on light fantastic toe
(Colossal monsters) for their dusky lord,
Who but the gods could such a sport afford?

* Ep. 326.

But all the rest is nothing, to compare
With lions taught to chase the timid hare.
They loose, recapture and caress their prey,
He feels at home, the deadly fangs make way,
Fearing to crush and mangle such small deer,
When fresh from slaughter of a lusty steer.
This training art alone cannot display;
The lions know their master and obey.

54 (I. cvii)

My dearest Julius, oft you say to me,
"Write something big." You're idle and you're free.
Give me true leisure, such as Virgil blessed
And Horace, in Maecenas' halls caressed.
Then will I soar and build the lofty rhyme,
Then from my ashes live in after time.
No steer o'er barren sands will drag his feet;
Fat soil is tiring, but the labour's sweet.

55 (I. cviii)

A mansion fair you have, long may it stand,
But, oh! far off beyond the Tiber strand.
My humble lodging fronts Agrippa's bay,
And in this quarter I grow old and grey.
So I must shift, my duty to fulfil;
'Tis worth my while, though you were further still.
To you 'tis nought to lose one morning call,
To miss my work to me is all in all.
At four o'clock my face you'll often see;
My book must pay my morning courtesy.

56 (I. cix)

Issa's more pert than Lesbia's sparrow love,
Purer than kisses of a turtle-dove,
More sweet than hundred maidens rolled in one,
Rarer than wealthy India's precious stone.
She is the pet of Publius, Issa dear;
She whines, a human voice you seem to hear.
Sorrow she knows and joy; with scarce a breath
She'll slumber on his breast as still as death.
If nature claims relief, she'll not offend
But with a gentle touch this message send,
"Drop me" or "lift me." For her chaste estate
'Twere passing hard to find a fitting mate.
Then, lest the grave fond memory's record raze,
Publius her living likeness here displays.
So like it is, this masterpiece of art,
Issa's less like herself, when they're apart.
Place dog and portrait side by side, you'll swear
Two Issas or two pictured forms were there.

57 (I. cxi)

Famed as you are for work and wisdom true
And piety to match the other two,
My Regulus, this book, this incense take;
Gifts more appropriate no hand can make.

58 (I. cxiii)

These trifles of my youth and fancies vain
That I myself scarce recognize again,
If you would cast your precious hours away
And cut to waste your hours of holiday,

At Polius the bookseller's you'll find;
He will not let my follies pass from mind.

59 (I. cxiv)

These gardens near, Faustinus, that you see
And oozy meads are Faenius' property.
Here is Antulla's name, his daughter, dead;
Poor child, she perished in her father's stead.
The sire should first have crossed the Stygian wave,
But fate forbade. He lives to tend her grave.

60 (I. cxv)

A JEALOUS LOVER

A whiter lassie dotes your bard upon
Than silver, lily, privet, snow or swan.
But I'm devoted to a coal-black maid, a
Darker than ant, pitch, jackdaw or cicada.
To the fell noose you thought your neck to give;
Procillus, if I know you well, you'll live.

61 (I. cvi)

In this fair garden and this hallowed grove
Faenius enshrined his daughter and his love.
Here lies Antulla, death's untimely prey,
And here shall Time her parents' ashes lay.
If any crave the plot, let him forbear;
Its lawful owners dwell for ever there.

62 (I. cxvii)

We never meet but you the phrase rehearse
"I'll send a boy to borrow of your verse,
Read and return it." Spare your boy for me;
My home ascends by lofty stages three,

Out by the Pear-tree. There's a quicker way.
You go by Argiletum every day.
By Caesar's Close a bookshop faces you
With all the poets in a bird's-eye view;
My name's among them, so you needn't stop
To ask Atrectus, owner of the shop.
He'll give you from some handy pigeon-hole
Polished and bound the handsome purple scroll.
For florins twain a copy he supplies.
"Too dear," you say. Lupercus, you are wise.

63 (II. i)

Three hundred epigrams were meet for you,
My book, but who would bear to read you through?
Now hear the merits of a Spartan taste;
Well, first so much less paper goes to waste.
Next, my good pen less time for drafting asks,
That leaves him leisure for more serious tasks.
Third, if some reader chance to look you o'er,
Bad though you be, you'll never be a bore.
A thirsty guest will finish you, I think,
Before his wine is cool enough to drink.
You deem such thrift of words will never weary;
Alas! how many still will find you dreary!

64 (II. ii)

ON THE SURNAME OF DOMITIAN

Metellus won a mighty name from Crete,
A mightier Scipio* from his foe's defeat,
　　* Conqueror of Hannibal.

More proud Germanicus from conquered Rhine;
Caesar, so fair a praise in boyhood's thine.
Judaea's bays thy sire and brother own;
The Dacian, Caesar, are for thee alone.

65 (II. iii)

You are no debtor, one and all we say,
He only owes, who has the power to pay.

66 (II. v)

Believe me, Decianus, when I say
That fain I would be with you night and day.
But 'tis two thousand paces, door to door;
Add the return trip and that makes it four.
You're often out or, when you're in, denied,
And with yourself or business occupied.
Two miles to see you I would gladly trot,
But four and then to miss you—ask me not!

67 (II. vi)

You bid me publish epigrams; go to!
Scarce have you read the first two pages through,
You pull long yawns, Severus, and you ask
"When comes the period to my doleful task?"
These verses, when I read them t'other day,
You'ld snatch and copy out on tablets gay.
These are the verses you could bear about
Next to your heart to theatre and rout.
They're here—and better, that you know not yet.
Small thanks do I for my conciseness get,

What though my book be meagre as the stick,
If it take three whole days the sense to pick!
Ne'er were pet verses read more leisurely.
A lazy traveller you seem to be;
Instead of trotting briskly to Bovillae
The "Muses"* tire you. Publish? Why, 'tis silly.

* A half-way house on a short journey from Rome.

68 (II. vii)

A pretty speech you make, a pretty plea,
A pretty verse, a pretty history.
In mime and epigram you're pretty smart,
In grammar, and in astrologic art.
'Tis pretty, too, the way you dance and sing,
And hurl the ball and wake the tuneful string
With all so pretty, nothing to applaud;
I tell you what you are—a pretty fraud.

69 (II. viii)

If any solecism or phrase obscure
Lurk in these poems, reader, then be sure
The blunder is not mine; my penman set 'em
Too roughly down, in haste for you to get 'em.
But, if you think I made the slip, not he,
Your want of judgment that can only be.
"But they're such rubbish." Why, the thing is clear
They're bad. You'll write no better ones, I fear.

70 (II. xi)

If Selius' brow all clouded o'er you mark
And if he haunts the cloisters in the dark;

If his sad face some dismal secret veils,
If on the ground his ugly trunk he trails;
He mourns not friend or brother, oh dear no;
They live and thrive, I trust they'll long do so.
His wife, kit, slaves are well as well can be,
No steward or bailiff plunged in bankruptcy.
What is his gloom and sorrow all about?
The reason's plain, he is not dining out.

71 (II. xiii)

If you don't pay old Shylock at once when you may,
You'll have counsel, judge, jury, Jew, devil to pay.

72 (II. xiv)

Selius leaves nought unventured, nought untried,
As often as at home he's forced to bide.
Off to Europa, where he pours his meed
Of praise, Paulinus, on your lightning speed.
Europa fails, then to the Booths he'll steal,
Jason or Chiron may provide a meal.
Baffled again, to Memphis' shrine* he goes
And loiters, doleful heifer, by your rows.
Next, to the hundred-pillared walk he'll shift
And twofold precinct, famous Pompey's gift†.
Nor then the humblest boiling bath he spurns,
To Gryllus' ‡ gloom and Faustus' wind-trap turns.
Then to Europa's box-wood once again,
In case some friend has missed the midnight train.

* The temple of Isis near the above. Most of the places are in
  or near the Campus Martius.
† The porch of Pompey with a wood on either side.
‡ Bath keepers.

Now, wanton bull*, by you and by your freight,
Give him a meal, good ferryman, ere too late.
* That carried Europa across the Hellespont.

73 (II. xvi)

Poor Zoilus* sickens. His bed's his excuse;
Were he well, he would find for his purple no use.
Rugs reeking from India, or mattress from Nile—
How else can a rich man exhibit his pile?
Disestablish your doctors, your health will be fine.
To keep it, you only need bedding like mine.
* A parvenu, once a slave.

74 (II. xvii)

A barber wench's booth Suburra sees,
Where cruel scourges float upon the breeze
And Argiletum leaves no passage through
Its manufactories of boot and shoe.
This barber, Ammianus, it appears,
Won't shave at all. What does she then? She shears.

75 (II. xviii)

I fish for dinner elsewhere, it is true,
But we are only quits, for so do you.
I pay a morning call, but you, 'tis plain,
Have been before me, so we're quits again.
I am the henchman, footman of your pride,
You of another's, so we're side by side.
I'll be a slave, but not the slave of one;
Who serves a king, he, Maximus, is none.

76 (II. xxiv)

If fortune, frowning, your good name should brand,
A paler culprit by your side I'll stand.
If she pronounce your banishment, I'll brave
With you the perils of the rock and wave.
She smiles. Have I no part in your success?
A thousand shocks you; I would take much less.
In trouble, Candidus, you need not doubt me,
But when you're happy, you can do without me.

77 (II. xxvii)

Reciting a poem or pleading a cause
You'll always find Selius prompt with applause.
He's scouting for dinner. "Smart! Witty! Bravo!"
Your dinner is earned and your gabble may go.

78 (II. xxix)

Rufus, see yonder in the foremost tier
Him with the ring that flashes right down here.
His mantle has drunk deep of Tyrian dye,
And with untrodden snow his coat may vie.
A whole perfumer's shop besmears his hair,
His clean-plucked arms are shining white and bare.
Upon his shoe each night the new moon* sits,
And lustrous scarlet, without galling, fits.
His brow's aglow with patches. Can you tell
The reason why? Take off the patches. Well?†

* A crescent on a scarlet shoe was part of a senator's full dress.
† FVR (thief) is branded underneath.

79 (II. xxx)

I asked you twenty thousand as a loan,
A trifle, had I craved it for my own,
Such claim might ancient friendship well afford
On one whose coffers chid their bursting hoard.
"Plead and you'll make a fortune in a trice."
I want your money, Gaius, not advice.

80 (II. xxxv)

With shin-bones like a crescent you were born;
Well might you bathe them in a drinking-horn.

81 (II. xxxvi)

You need not curl your hair; but why so rough?
And, for your skin, a bath were wash enough.
No prisoner's head nor yet vizier's I'ld scan,
Neither too little nor too much a man.
In boar's accoutrements you play your part,
But you're a rabbit, Pannychus, at heart.

2 (II. xxxvii)

Boar helpings set for neighbours where you dine,
A whole sow's udder or a porker's chine,
Perhaps a woodcock that two guests might like
Or half a mullet or a solid pike,
A lamprey fillet or a pullet's thigh
And fatted pigeon simmering in its fry,
All these into your dripping napkin ooze;
The boy will fetch them when he brings your shoes
We sit and gaze. For shame, the feast repay;
I asked you not to-morrow but to-day.

83 (II. xxxviii)

You ask of my Nomentan farm
How such a barren waste can charm.
One reason is, I find no trace
There, Linus, of your ugly face.

85 (II. xl)

Tongilius is very sick to-day
Of a quotidian fever. That's his way.
For fatted fieldfares now he lies in wait
Or for a pike or mullet sets his bait.
Draw Caecuban and rich Opimian wine,
Or dark Falernian's thrifty* cups divine†.
"The man must bathe," this bulletin you read.
Oh fool, you think it fever. 'Tis his greed.

* Small cups used for strong wine.
† To prevent a chill in bathing.

86 (II. xli)

"Smile, maiden, smile" was Ovid's counsel sage,
But not addressed to girls of any age.
Or, if it was, it was not meant for you,
It is for others; you are old, not new,
And the three teeth that still adorn your face
With pitch or box-wood might secure a place.
So, if my counsel and the glass you trust,
You'll shrink from mirth as Spanius from each gust
Of wind, as Priscus dreads a finger-stain,
As fears Fabulla's powdered cheek the rain
Or bleached Sabella blinks at morning sun.
Then pull a solemn face whate'er the fun;

Like Priam's spouse or prude Andromache,
Shunning Philistion's boisterous ribaldry
And jolly banquets where infectious chaff
Spreads wide our features with a joyous laugh.
Lest through your smile the treacherous daylight peep,
Take my advice and weep, dear maiden, weep.

87 (II. xliii)

"Friends share alike" is still your cuckoo-cry,
By day and night it greets the passer-by.
This, though your robe was in Galaesus * dipt,
Or from the choicest flock of Parma clipt,
While mine has seen a savage bull's attack
And would disgrace a modest scarecrow's back!
In purple Tyrian mantles you appear,
My cloak at half-a-crown would sell too dear.
Your board's upreared on Indian ivory,
A crock-borne table's good enough for me.
Your gold intaglio fat mullet hides,
Red crab with my red platter coincides.
In all your wealth an ancient friend and true
Receives no portion. "Share alike," say you?

* A river of S. Italy famous for sheep-pastures.

88 (II. xliv)

I buy a varlet or a garment new
Or spice or pepper, say a pound or two,
Good banker Sextus, that old friend of mine—
You know, he's in the money-lending line—
Conceiving I might intimate a loan,
Says to himself but not in whispering tone,

"Seven thousand due Secundus heads the score,
Eleven to Philetus, Phoebus four;
And then I've not a farthing in my chest."
Oh subtle wit, O comrade faithfullest!
To ask is nothing and receive a snub;
But not to ask and get one, there's the rub.

89 (II. xlvi)

As Hybla flaunts in nature's colouring,
While bees invade the brief Sicilian spring,
So do your presses gleam with cloaks in piles,
Your chest is gay with countless dinner styles.
White robes sufficient half the town to dress
The pride of two Apulian flocks express.
Ah! wretch, unmerciful to comrade old,
You shun the contact of his mantle cold.
A simple thing to spare a scrap of cloth,
When you would not have missed it, but the moth.

90 (II. liii)

You want your freedom, Maximus? Not so;
But, should you want it, here's the way to go.
Can you dispense with going out to dine,
And quench your thirst with modest Veientine;
Cinna's intaglio shepherds blithely miss
And be contented with a coat like this?
If such your force, your spirit's tempering,
You'll have more freedom than the Parthian king.

91 (II. lvii)

This fellow, lounging through the crowded fair,
Decked out in amethystine mantle rare,
Who might with feasting Publius find a place
Or Cordus, arbiter of outdoor grace,
Whose train have flowing locks and robes of white,
Whose litter, straps and linen linings bright,
The other day, for dinner's whole expense,
Raised on his ring a grudging fifteen pence.

92 (II. lviii)

Oh yes, you may smile in your garment so fine
At this shabby mantle. It's old, but it's mine.

93 (II. lix)

Men call me Jewel, tiny banquet-room;
The pile that fronts thee is great Caesar's tomb*.
Lie soft, anoint thee, crown the bowl with roses;
This shrine the warrant of thy death discloses.

* The Mausoleum of Augustus.

94 (II. lxiv)

Now you would pleader be, now orator,
And can't decide what you are fitted for.
Peleus and Priam's span and Nestor's age
Are past; 'twere even late to leave the stage.
Begin; three schools are silent since last year—
If you have heart or wit for that career.

You damn the schools, the law-courts are aglow;
Marsyas'* self might play the pleader so.
Come! make a dash and end our expectation;
You'll come to grief with "What is my vocation?"

* A statue in the law-courts.

95 (II. lxv)

Why's Saleianus so depressed to-day?
"I've buried my poor wife. Good cause," you say.
Oh grievous stroke! Oh sad calamity!
What, dead? The wealthy Secundilla? She
Who to your money-chest her million brought?
You have my sympathy, I'm sure you ought.

96 (II. lxvi)

Of her fair locks one gadding tress had strayed,
Fixed by the hairpin of a careless maid.
Lalage saw the crime; the glass was there.
Plecusa fell, struck by the mirrored hair*.
Ne'er, Lalage, those felon tresses twine,
Ne'er maiden hand that frenzied brow confine.
Let lizard brand them or fell razor hack;
An ugly mask the mirror will give back.

* *I.e.*, the mirror itself.

97 (II. lxviii)

If I address you by your name, no more,
Instead of "lord and master" as before,
Don't think me churlish, but make light of it;
I bought this liberty with all my kit.

He is a servant, and deserves to be,
Who has not in himself sufficiency,
But, like his lord and master, help requires
To gain the object that his soul desires.
If man can do without an underling,
Olus, he well may do without a king.

98 (II. lxix)

You say you so detest to dine abroad,
Now hang me, Classicus, but you're a fraud.
Even Apicius* loved to go about;
Because he felt so dull at home, no doubt.
Why go at all then, if you make a fuss?
"Why, I can't help it!" Nor can Selius†.
Melior invites you to a spread to go;
Where is your talk? If you're a man, say no.

* A millionaire.   † A parasite.

99 (II. lxxi)

Your candour, Caecilianus, well I know.
Hear but a couplet of my verse or so,
Straight Marsus* or Catullus you recite;
A gracious tribute, "they're inferior quite."
Perhaps you want the contrast to be shown;
If that be so, you'ld better read your own.

* He wrote Virgil's epitaph.

100 (II. lxxiv)

See, round Saufeius and behind, a crowd
Of which a Regulus* might well be proud,

* A great advocate.

Whose client stands before the altar shorn*.
Don't envy him; he more deserves your scorn.
Matinus, be you ne'er escorted so,
Nor any of your dear ones! 'Tis but show;
This white-clad retinue, these troops of friends
Not his profession but his banker lends†.

* To give thanks for his acquittal.
† He paid them to come and borrowed money.

101 (II. lxxv)

A lion, broken to his lord's command
And trained to suffer his controlling hand,
In savage fit forgot his gentle ways
And turned more fierce than in his Libyan days,
Burst through the crowd that swept the blood-stained floor
And two poor lads in barbarous fury tore.
Fie on thee, treacherous beast, unkind, unfair!
Our own she-wolf* had taught thee youth to spare.

* Who suckled Romulus and Remus.

102 (II. lxxvii)

Cosconius, you, who would abridge my lay,
Might grease a wheel with credit any day.
By such account Colossus is too tall,
The Boy* of Brutus on a scale too small.
Marsus and Pedo—it is time you learned—
Will often end before a page is turned.
Nothing is long when nothing is to spare,
But you write lengthy couplets unaware.

* A statuette.

103 (II. lxxxi)

Though bearers six upon thy litter wait,
A hearse, poor Zoilus, is all thy state*.

* Zoilus, a parvenu, is socially a dead man. Comp. Ep. 73.

104 (II. lxxxv)

A wicker basket water cool to guard,
That is my Christmas gift. You think it hard?
You don't like summer presents in December?
Send me a summer toga* then, remember.

* *I.e.*, of fine texture.

105 (II. lxxxvi)

I've no delight in topsy-turvy verse,
Nor backwards dirty Sotades rehearse;
I love not Attis'* galliambic strain
For greekling echo to repeat again.
Yet I'm a poet. Ladas† would you ask
To scale a slippery spring-board as a task?
'Tis hard bewildering riddles to compose
And labour lost to work at nonsense prose.
For vulgar readers let Palaemon write;
The educated few are my delight.

* A poem of Catullus.   † The famous race-horse.

106 (II. xc)

AN EXCUSE FOR INDOLENCE

Consummate guide of youth's capricious way,
Quintilian*, hero of the legal fray,

* The great advocate and teacher.

Young blood will have its course; my haste forgive;
Methinks it never is too soon to live.
Let him put off, who would his sires outvie,
And crowd his halls with cumbrous pageantry;
Give me a hearth, a smoky ingle nook,
And live green turf beside the babbling brook,
A fat-cheeked slave, a wife not wise all ways,
Nights of repose and unlitigious days.

107 (II. xci)

Great prince, upholder of our sovereignty,
Whose welfare bids us know the gods to be,
If in my verse a line or two appear,
Caesar, appealing to your sovereign ear,
Suffer to seem what truth and fate deny,
That I am father of a family*.
Then, if I fail, this fraud will give me ease,
'Twill be my bounteous guerdon, if I please.

* Entitling him to certain privileges; see Ep. 501.

108 (II. xcii)

The three-child-father-dole was my petition;
The All-highest winked and gave my suit admission.
Well ta-ta, wife; you're useless, go and play;
My sovereign's bounty's not to throw away.

109 (III. i)

Better or worse, these rhymes are sent to town
From Gaul, god-daughter of the Roman gown*.

* *I.e.*, Northern Italy, not yet Lombardy, which had Gallic blood and
  Roman dress.

You like the old work better than the new?
I'll own as mine whatever pleases you.
The Roman product you may well prefer;
A home-bred slave should beat the foreigner.

110 (III. ii)

Quick, claim a sponsor, or you'll feed the cook,
Or spice or pepper hold, beloved book,
Or else envelop greasy whitebait fries.
You haste to name Faustinus; well, you're wise.
Now, cedar-scented, you may blithely stray
With graceful frontlets and with bosses gay;
Of purple grain shall be your dainty shell,
Your name and matter blushing scarlet tell.
By him attested, no detraction fear;
Probus* is silent with Faustinus near.

* A critic.

111 (III. iv)

To Rome, my book. If she asks whence, you'll say,
"From the direction of the Aemilian way*."
Demand she in what town I am and where;
Say that I'm staying at Cornelius' Fair.
"Why am I absent?" Say, "Attendance palls
And liveried vanity of morning calls."
"And when returning?" Answer, "He left Rome
A poet; when a harper† he'll come home."

* From Bononia southwards.
† Musicians were better paid than poets.

112 (III. v)

Good-bye, my book. And which will suit you better?
To one or many shall I write a letter?
One man will give you hospitality,
Julius*, familiar household word with me.
Forthwith you'll seek him in the Covered Way;
Daphnis lived here, 'tis Julius' home to-day.
He has a wife, who'll give you welcome home,
Though hot and dusty from the road you come.
Husband or wife, whichever first you're meeting,
You'll say, "My master gives you kindly greeting."
Enough. A letter strangers' worth commends.
No man wants introducing to his friends.

* Cerealis.

113 (III. vi)

Yours, Marcellinus, is the mid-May feast,
Of anniversaries not honoured least;
Twice happy, 'twas your father's natal day
And your cheek's tribute did to manhood pay*.
For this the father more his birthday owed
Than all the happiness that birth bestowed.

* The first cutting of the beard.

114 (III. vii)

You poor old hundred farthings, you may trudge*,
Fit largess of a weary footman drudge;
The parboiled bathman took a goodly share;
How now, my comrades, can we live on air?
Our patron's service brings us no reward;
What's his alternative? To pay our board.

* The client's dole, now replaced by a dinner which was its original
form. The change proved a failure; see Ep. 120, 132.

115 (III. viii)

> Quintus dotes on Thais,
>   Eye has she but one;
> All that can I say is
>   That her swain has none.

116 (III. x)

> Your father, Philomusus, gave to you
> Two thousand sesterces, for monthly due.
> To-day's full gorging meant to-morrow's need
> And daily doles must satisfy your greed.
> Dying he left you all his wealth instead.
> Alack, my boy, you're disinherited!

117 (III. xi)

AN APOLOGY FOR EP. 115

> I called her Thais, and your one-eyed flame.
> If she was neither, I am not to blame.
> "A name disguised?" Yes; Lais it should be;
> But how could Thais mean Hermione?
> One alteration. Quintus can't be right;
> Quintus does not love Thais; Sextus might.

118 (III. xii)

> Your perfumes yesterday were good,
> But then, you droll, you gave no food;
>   We starved mid odours gummy.
> Pray tell me, at a funeral feast
> Who smells the most and eats the least,
>   Fabullus? Why, the mummy.

119 (III. xiii)

You don't like the fish, of the fowl you'll have none,
And you turn up your nose at the rags of a boar;
You scold your poor cook and you beat him till sore;
The meat may be raw, but your guests are well done

120 (III. xiv)

The same as 114.

Hungry Tuccius came to Rome,
But at the Bridge, alack oh!
"The dole is dead," they cried, and home
He trotted hungry back, oh!

121 (III. xv)

None gives more on credit than Cordus, you'll find.
What, is he so poor? No, he loves and is blind.

122 (III. xvi)

Good prince of cobblers, you give fighting shows;
What the awl brings you by the dagger goes.
You're drunk, my friend; no sober man would sin
Against his judgment, gambling with his skin.
Cobbler, take my advice; give up your pride;
Stick to the last; in your own skin abide.

123 (III. xviii)

"You must excuse my tragic muse
Strained from a husky chest."
Oh pray, sir, don't, we beg you won't;
Give your poor throat a rest.

124 (III. xix)

    Nigh to the Hundred Columns stands a bear
    By veiling plane-trees mantled everywhere.
    The pretty Hylas, keeping holiday,
    Sounded its open mouth in daring play.
    A deadly viper lurked within the maw,
    A foe more fatal than the monster's paw.
    Death struck; too late he knew the sculptured snare
    And in the serpent missed the gentler bear.

125 (III. xx)

    Tell me, my muse, how Rufus spends his time.
    Tells he of Claudius in deathless rhyme,
    Or fabled Nero, or to Phaedrus sly
    Inclines his fancy, or to Epic high
    Or wanton Elegiac? Does his page
    Play Sophocles and strut the buskined stage,
    Or does he in the poets' club-room sit
    And tell gay stories spiced with Attic wit?
    Sated with these, perchance to the portico
    And Argonautic lounge he'll idly go.
    Or in Europa's box-wood does he rest,
    Or walk and bask, by no grave care oppressed?
    Plunge in Agrippa's, Titus' bath, or cool
    His limbs in shameless Tigellinus' pool?
    With Tullus, Lucan, make his country home
    Or Polio's pleasant farm four miles from Rome?
    Beneath the spell of Baiae does he fall,
    Or float the Lucrine lake? He laughs; that's all.

126 (III. xxi)

The branded slave who saved his master's head
Not life but fires of retribution fed.

127 (III. xxii)

Some thirty millions* to your appetite
You gave and had to spare two millions quite.
Starvation! So you drained the deadly cup.
Your life was greediest at its winding up.

* Of sesterces, nearly £250,000.

128 (III. xxiii)

You hand your fine dishes to slaves for removal;
A Barmecide's table would meet your approval.

129 (III. xxv)

Faustinus, if your boiling bath you'ld cool
Enough to banish Julian* from the pool,
Ask Sabinaeus in; his lectures will,
I warrant, give e'en Nero's baths the chill.

* A fop.

130 (III. xxvii)

My hospitality goes unrequited;
A trifle, Gallus, were but others slighted;
But no, you ask them. We are both to blame;
I have no sense and, Gallus, you no shame.

131 (III. xxix)

Saturn, these gyves he offers to your praise,
Poor Zoilus, his rings of other days*.

* He had been a slave; see Ep. 73.

132 (III. xxx)
See Ep. 30 and 114.

> You dine but have no pence; no dole is due.
> Gargilianus, what is Rome to you?
> How get your threadbare coat and cubby hole?
> For both and light-of-love you miss the dole.
> You say "you live on rations." Can you call
> It rational in you to live at all?

133 (III. xxxi)

> You're lord of many acres, I've no doubt,
> A hundred freeholds fence your house about.
> A hundred debtors on your bounty wait
> And your rich feast's upborne by massive plate.
> Yet do not to the poor your scorn display.
> Eunuchs had more, a harpist has to-day.

134 (III. xxxvi)

> The service of an unfledged, new-hatched friend,
> This, Fabianus, you would have me lend;
> To go unkempt my patron's house to greet
> Through the poached filth that floods the middle street;
> To Agrippa's bath at four to wait on you,
> Worn out, or later, when I've bathed at two,
> This the reward that thirty winters brought?
> Dwell I but in the suburbs of your thought?
> What boots it for this threadbare gown to pay*,
> If I've not earned dismissal by to-day?

> * The toga, which was the necessary full dress for attendance on
> a patron.

135 (III. xxxviii)

What cause or confidence brings you to Rome?
What do you hope or wish for? Tell me, come.
"I'll plead more learnedly than Cicero;
No prouder name shall court or client know."
Civis and Atestinus both did that,
And neither's home holds space to swing a cat.
"All failing, I'll write poems. Hear me sing,
You'ld think that Epic Virgil plucked the string."
You're mad. The tatters of his cloak betray
The Ovid or the Virgil of to-day.
"I'll court rich patrons." Three or four, I'm told,
Can live like that, the rest are starved and cold.
"I mean to live there; you suggest a plan."
Live? You've small chance, if you're an honest man.

136 (III. xl)

You lent me three fifties*, my friend, and no more
From all the vast wealth of your manifold store.
You think yourself loyal. "There's friendship!" you're
    saying.
The friendship is surely my own in repaying.

* Say £1.

137 (III. xliii)

You play the youth with raven hue assumed,
But yesterday like swan of Leda plumed.
Not all you cheat; Proserpine knows you grey.
Some day she'll pluck your silly mask away.

138 (III. xliv)

That no one, Ligurinus, likes to meet
Your visage, that there's panic in the street
At your approach, the reason, would you know it?
Well, Ligurinus, you're too much a poet.
A grievous fault, with perilous mischief fraught.
No tigress, for her captive brood distraught,
Puff-adder sweltering in the noon-tide heat,
Or ruthless scorpion is so dread to meet.
Who can endure it? Standing, in repose,
Your strain pursues me; while I bathe it flows.
I seek the swimming-pool; no refuge there.
I haste to dinner; there's another scare.
Weary I sleep; you wake me. What's your error?
Just, righteous, harmless, you're a holy terror.

139 (III. xlv)

Round Atreus' board did Phoebus draw a curtain?
Yours, Ligurinus, we avoid, that's certain.
Rich may the dinner be and sumptuous quite,
It cannot satisfy while you recite.
Let turbot, mushroom, two-pound mullet cease;
Oysters I crave not, but to dine in peace.

140 (III. xlvi)

You ask for slavish service without end.
No, I'll not come, a freedman I will send.
"'Tis not the same," you say; 'tis more, I swear;
I should precede your litter, he will bear.
His elbow stout will thrust the crowd aside;
I am a weakling, but with Roman pride.

When you are pleading, I shall hold my peace;
He'll shout the loud bravo and never cease.
Should brawl arise, he'll scold at any rate,
I am ashamed to deal in Billingsgate.
"Is there no office, then, a friend may fill?"
Whate'er a freedman cannot, that I will.

141 (III. xlvii)

Where with great drops the Capuan gate's adrip
And Cybele's priests her knives in Almo dip
To where thy sacred meads, Horatius, press
The busy fane of Hercules the less*;
Faustinus, with full cart see Bassus ride
Bearing the spoils of the rich country-side.
There you might see the cabbage bushy-polled,
Squat lettuces and leeks both young and old,
The wholesome beet, fieldfares on withy bound
And hare, torn victim of a Gallic hound.
A sucking pig, as yet of beans afraid,
Came last. A part the honest carter played
And carried eggs in hay kept snug and warm.
Bassus was townward bent? No, to his farm.

* Domitian was the greater Hercules; see Ep. 505 n.

142 (III. xlviii)

OLUS' "FOLLY"

Olus, to build a "poor man's cote,"
Sold all, so that's what now he's got.

143 (III. l)

For this your guests to supper you invite,
That you your nonsense verses may recite.
Off go my shoes and straight ere one can look
With sauce and salad comes a ponderous book.
Another's brought, and the first course deferred,
And ere dessert is ready, comes a third.
Again a fourth and still the cry is "more";
A taint accompanies perpetual boar.
If you don't give your rubbish to the fishes
You'll have no company for books or dishes.

144 (III. lii)

You bought a house, Tongilianus, dear;
'Twas gutted by a fire, too common here.
You raised—a fortune. Someone might suppose
That through your handiwork the flame arose.

145 (III. lv)

Where'er you're wafted, Cosmos seems to pass
And sprinkle balsams from an upturned glass.
Don't be too proud of foreign odours rich;
This perfume would lend fragrance to my bitch.

146 (III. lvi)

ON THE SCARCITY OF WATER AT RAVENNA

Your tanks for me, Ravenna, not your vines;
The waters I can sell, but not the wines.

147 (III. lvii)
The same.

> The man who sold wine at Ravenna's a cheat;
> I asked for it watered; he gave me it neat.

148 (III. lviii)

> Faustinus' farm, dear Bassus, is arrayed
> With no luxurious groves of olive shade.
> No wood of bachelor plane*, no facile box
> The thankless acres of his garden mocks.
> It smiles, a rural and a wild retreat;
> Here Ceres' bounty right and left you meet.
> Ripe teems the fragrant jar; till winter's date
> The unkempt pruner gathers clusters late.
> In the deep valleys hear the angry cattle;
> The unhorned calf is spoiling for the battle.
> The chicken-yard sends forth its dusty crowd,
> The cackling goose, the jewelled peacock proud,
> The red flamingo, pencilled guinea-hen,
> Partridge or pheasant reared by godless men†.
> The Rhodian cock is there and all around
> Dovecotes with pigeons' flapping wings resound.
> The waxen turtle and the stock-dove coo
> And greedy pigs the farm-wife's apron woo.
> Lambs for their mothers bleat; in festal rays
> Bask infant slaves, the woodlands feed the blaze.
> No cellarer here sits limp and putty-faced,
> No slippery gymnast calls for oil to waste;
> For greedy felts they spread a wily snare
> Or draw the finny prey with quivering hair.

* Not used, like the elm, for training vines.
† In Colchis, the country of Medea.

4–2

The town-bred slaves work the kind garden round;
No crabbed martinet will there be found;
The long-haired rascals greet the bailiff's cry,
The unmanly eunuch loves his task to ply.
There comes to call no idle country fellow,
In its own comb is borne the honey yellow.
A cone of cheese is there from Sassina's wood,
A slave boy shows a sleepy dormouse brood,
One of a hairy goat the bleating young;
A fifth, a bachelor capon brings along.
Tall maids of honest cottage neighbours bear
Their mother's gift in woven basket-ware.
When work is done, troop in the neighbours gay
No churlish saving for another day;
Enough for all; and a contented drudge
The festive wine-cup will not nicely judge.
A suburb's prim privation is your fare;
Look down; no robbers haunt your laurels bare;
Your vineyard staff on city corn must dine;
To idle halls you bring eggs, poultry, wine,
Fruit, cheese and vegetables. Did you say
"A country house"? A town house gone astray.

149 (III. lx)

Your pensioner no longer*, but your guest,
Why at your table am I grudged the best?
Fat Lucrine oysters wait upon your need,
A half-oped mussel makes my palate bleed.
Mushrooms your platter, mine vile toad-stools fill
Your meat's a turbot, mine ambitious brill.

* Ep. 30, 114.

The golden doves for you their rumps display,
My pauper's pittance is a sickly jay.
For loss of dole some compensation's due;
I share your table; let me dine with you.

150 (III. lxi)

Of your importunate request you cry
"'Tis nothing!" Nothing, Cinna, I deny.

151 (III. lxii)

You give a hundred thousand* for a page;
Your cellar's date ascends to Numa's age;
A million† for a simple suit you pay,
One pound of plate with thousands runs away.
Your gilded coach is worth a homestead's fee.
Your mule costs more than your new property.
You think this shows your spirit, but behind
Such ostentation lurks a feeble mind.

* £800.   † £8000.

152 (III. lxiii)

Yes, you're a pretty fellow; every one
Says so. What's "pretty," Cotilus, when all's done?
"A pretty fellow curls his locks with care,
Still primed with cinnamon and spices rare;
He'll murmur airs of Egypt, songs of Spain,
His smooth white arms afloat to many a strain,
And all day long to women's seats he's near
To whisper something no one else must hear.
He's reading notes or writing all the day,
And from your elbow draws his cloak away.

With gossip fraught from board to board he'll gad
And knows what ancestors Hirpinus* had."
Good Cotilus, if I your meaning share,
A "pretty fellow" is but flimsy ware.

* A horse.

153 (III. lxv)

Sweet as an apple bit by dainty maid
Or yellow vine in early bloom arrayed,
As saffron, myrtle, amber, cinnamon
Or flames with fragrant incense pale and wan,
As earth new moist with gentle rain in spring,
Or oozy locks with spikenard glistening,
So sweet, so fresh, your kisses are to me;
Would you but part with them less grudgingly.

154 (III. lxvi)

Antonius, rivalling the Egyptian crime*,
With his fell sword severed a head sublime.
One gained us laurels in victorious war;
The other was our matchless orator†.
Antonius' sin is fouler and more dire;
Pothinus served his master, he his ire.

* The murder of Pompey.   † Cicero.

155 (III. lxvii)

You're idle, mates, and ill your business know,
Idler than Rasina or Vaternus slow,
Upon whose languid current borne along
You dip your slow oars to the boatman's song.

With sweating steeds the sloping sun's afire,
And weary teams to noon-tide rest retire;
You on the placid wave go holidaying,
Not Argonauts but Argo-naughty playing.

156 (III. lxxvii)

Mullet or fieldfare, Baeticus, no more,
Nor hare has charm for you, nor stately boar.
No sweets or dainty cakes can give you ease,
Pheasant and guinea-fowl alike displease.
Capers and onions in fish-pickle stale
And questionable pork your soul regale.
Pale tunny and sardines a banquet grace,
And resined wines take old Falernian's place.
A man's complaint is hard to diagnose
Whose appetite is like a carrion crow's.

157 (III. xciv)

"Give me the whip! the hare's not fit to eat."
You'll rather flay your cook than carve your meat.

158 (III. xcix)

Good cobbler*, don't be angry with my ware,
Your craft and not your life is libelled there.
Suffer my harmless jests; can it be ill
For me to laugh, and right for you to kill?

* Ep. 122.

159 (III. c)

A WET BOOK FOR "WET" COMPANY

Compare Ep. 161, 210, 522.

> I'm sending you my verses by your lad;
>   He'll reach you somewhat wetter by and by;
> 'Tis twelve o'clock, and raining here like mad;
>   No matter; such a book should not go dry.

160 (IV. i)

DOMITIAN

> Birthday of Caesar, holier than the light
> That bare great Jove on conscious Ida's height,
> Dawn on us, linger age on age, I pray,
> Gleaming as fair or fairer than to-day.
> Here may he kneel in golden Pallas' shrine
> And many an oak-wreath grace those hands divine;
> Here the returning centuries review
> And celebrate Tarentos'* rites anew.
> Our plea is but the due of earth, though great;
> For such a god what prayer's importunate?

* Otherwise known as the Secular Games.

161 (IV. viii)

A ROMAN DAY

To the superintendent of Domitian's table.

> The first and second hours on friends we call,
> The third, we hear the husky pleader bawl,
> Until the fifth we rival ant or bee,
> The sixth we rest, the seventh and we go free.

The eighth with exercise and sunshine glows,
The ninth disturbs the banquet hall's repose,
The tenth, Euphemus, calls for verse of mine
While you inaugurate a feast divine.
Caesar, at rest, takes princely nectar up
And holds in his great hand a tiny cup.
Then for High Jinks. My playful muse, take warning,
Vex not the dreaded Thunderer in the morning.

162 (IV. x)

While yet my volume is unkempt and rough,
The page still bashful and not dry enough,
Boy, my small present to a dear friend bring
Well worthy of my simple offering.
Go, but equipped; let this be at thy side,
That can be aptly to my gifts applied.
A year's correcting will but prove me dunce;
A sponge obliterates all faults at once.

163 (IV. xi)

ANTONIUS SATURNINUS THE REBEL

Proud to be Antony*, though idly named,
And yet of Saturninus† half ashamed,
Beneath the Northern star you stir up strife
Like his who fought for an Egyptian wife.
Have you forgotten what a death he died
Whelmed by the fury of the Actian tide?
The Nile refused him what you ask of Rhine;
Is Rhenus greater than the flood divine?
The great Antonius Roman legions slew,
Himself a Caesar when compared with you.

* Antony the "triumvir."   † A democrat of republican days.

164 (IV. xiii)

Claudia's to marry Pudens, so they say.
God's blessing, Rufus, on their wedding day.
So cinnamon and spikenard will combine,
And Attic honey blend with Massic wine.
So with the vine the elm is mantled o'er,
So Lotus loves the wave, Myrtle the shore.
Unbroken union be their portion here
And Venus smile on wedded peer and peer.
May she still love him when her hair is grey,
To him as youthful as she is to-day.

165 (IV. xiv)

Silius, great bard, who with thy stately verse
The savage Punic treachery dost rehearse,
And biddest faithless Hannibal's perjury
To our great Scipio bow low the knee,
Be gay awhile, what time released from bounds
December's call the baffling dice-box sounds,
Or treacherous sleight deludes. Be kind to-day,
Nor frown upon a laughing poet's lay.
So greatly daring might Catullus send
His darling's sparrow to his poet friend*.

* Virgil.

166 (IV. xv)

You begged, Caecilianus, yesterday
A thousand sesterces*; next week you'ld pay.
Well, I refused, and now, because a friend
Is come, a dozen crocks I'm asked to lend.

* £8.

Are you a fool? Am I? Why, man alive,
A thousand I denied. Shall I give five?

167 (IV. xviii)

Hard by Agrippa's porch there stands a gate
    Oozing and slippery with still falling dew.
The leaden frost-bound waters sealed the fate
    Of a poor lad, who to the archway drew.
Scarce had the ice-flake wrought its deadly will,
    It melted in the boy's warm throat away.
If healthful waters have such power to kill,
    Where lurks not death? Who fortune's spite can stay?

168 (IV. xix)

I send a blanket with a Spartan name;
A coarse affair, from Gallia's loom it came.
'Tis not well-favoured, but may make a shift
To be a not unwelcome Christmas gift,
Whether in oily trim you try a fall
Or field or scramble for the dusty ball,
Or ponderous feather bag in concert ply
Or seek in running Athas to outvie.
Thus armed, no frost will riddle you with ague,
No sudden deluge from the sky will plague you.
Laughing at wind and rain alike you'll go.
A Tyrian mantle would not save you so.

169 (IV. xxi)

"There are no gods," says Segius, "and the blue
Is void." He lives and thrives and proves it true.

170 (IV. xxiii)

> While in your mind the question doubtful lies
> Who for Greek epigram deserves the prize,
> Callimachus has yielded up his claim
> And graced the palm with Brutianus' name.
> If, honey-cloyed, he to our Muse incline
> For pastime, let the second place be mine.

171 (IV. xxiv)

> Friends had Lycoris. She survives them all.
> Ah, Fabianus, if my wife would call!

172 (IV. xxv)

> Altinum, rival of the Baian coast,
> Wood where poor Phaethon was set to toast,
> Where Sola, fairest Dryad of the brake,
> Wed Faunus by the green Euganean lake;
> Blest Aquileia by Timavus bank,
> Where Cyllarus the seven-fold waters drank;
> You of mine age will be the haven blest
> If I may choose at last my place of rest.

173 (IV. xxvi)

> I find you "not at home" the whole year through;
> What lose I, Postumus? I'll tell you true.
> Twice thirty, three times twenty pence, we'll say.
> Forgive! My coat's more costly any day.

174 (IV. xxvii)

Caesar, you love to praise my little verse.
Envy says, "no." You love me none the worse.
Your single fiat has bestowed on me
Such gifts as from no other I could see.
Envy still gnaws his nails, again, again.
Give me the more, the more to give him pain.

175 (IV. xxx)

Haste, fisherman, from Baiae lake away!
Foul guilt thy company if thou delay.
Of sacred fish these waters are the home
Who kiss the hands supreme of earth and Rome.
Yet greater marvel, there are names for all
And each one answers to his master's call.
A poaching African with impious care
Drew forth his quarry on a quivering hair.
Swift judgment followed, for bereft of sight
His eye might not behold his booty bright.
And now he loves the thieving hook no more,
And sits a beggar by the Baian shore.
Stranger, take warning then, forbear to steal
And give the dainty fish an honest meal.

176 (IV. xxxii)

In amber drop enmeshed, a gadding bee,
Like a bright prisoner in her masonry,
Won rich reward for labours multiplied.
Methinks that even so she would have died.

177 (IV. xxxiii)

Sosibianus, though your library
Is full of careful work, we nothing see.
"My heirs will read it." Well then, off you go,
For your executors would have it so.

178 (IV. xxxiv)

Your toga, Attalus, is like the snow;
The feel and not the colour dubs it so.

179 (IV. xxxv)

We've seen the timid stags with antlers tall
Clash and alike in deadly duel fall.
The very hounds gazed at the unwonted strife;
Proud huntsmen marvelled while they sheathed the knife.
Where gat these gentle souls such chivalry?
So bulls will fight, so gladiators die.

180 (IV. xxxvii)

"Coranus owes a hundred*, two Mancinus,
Three hundred Titius, twice as much Albinus,
A million† from Sabinus is my due,
And then Sarranus, there is one from you.
My land brings in three millions every year,
And Parma's flocks six hundred thousand clear."
Day in day out, your story's still the same;
I know it better than I know my name.
Give something, health and patience to restore;
I cannot listen gratis any more.

  100,000 sesterces—£800.   † £8000.

181 (IV. xxxix)

Carinus, you've amassed all kinds of plate,
And Myron's masterpieces deck your state.
Scopas, Praxiteles, for yours you claim,
Mentor and Phidias, 'tis all the same.
You've vessels dear of Gratianus old
And costly goblets lined with Spanish gold.
You've priceless vases, heirlooms handed down
And yet, how strange, no shilling of your own.

182 (IV. xl)

The halls of Piso stood with family tree,
And Seneca's house with three-fold ancestry.
We loved you more, for all their regal state;
To me at least a lowly knight was great.
We shared some thirty winters, you and I,
And on one couch together we would lie.
Now you are rich, you've plenty and to spare;
I'm all attention. Postumus, my share!
It is too late a stranger's bread to eat,
Fie on it, Postumus! you are a cheat.

183 (IV. xli)

Why when reciting swathe with wool your head?
Such mufflings better suit our ears instead.

184 (IV. xliv)

THE ERUPTION OF VESUVIUS IN A.D. 79

Vesuvius here was green with mantling vine,
Here brimming vats o'erflowed with noble wine.

These hills to jocund Bacchus were more dear
Than Nysa, and the Satyrs revelled here.
This blest retreat could Cytherea please,
This owned the fame of godlike Hercules;
Now dismal ashes all and scorching flame.
Such dire caprice might move a god to shame.

185 (IV. xlv)
For Parthenius, see Ep. 217.

To-day Parthenius of the Palatine
Lays joyful offerings, Phoebus, at thy shrine.
For Burrus, son of fifteen years, he prays
That he may fill innumerable days.
Grant thou his prayer. So love thee well thy tree,
Thy sister boast her deathless chastity.
Thus may'st thou bloom for ever, nor thy hair
Confess the wine-god's clustering locks more fair.

186 (IV. xlvi)
Presents from clients took the place of advocates' fees which were not lawful.

Sabellus has acquired a competence
This Christmas. In his boast there is some sense.
"There's not a lawyer man in all the land
Richer than I am, you shall understand."
Of shredded beans and pulse he'll show you sacks,
Black pepper, incense by the pound, nor lacks
Lucanian sausages, Faliscan chine,
And Syrian flask of desiccated wine.
With these, a Libyan crystal cake of fig
And truffles, snails and cheese, he's mighty big.
A client from Picenum sends a jar
Of thrifty olive from her home afar.

Seven cups from famed Saguntum on the board
A sample of the potter's art afford.
His napkin's purple, round a sober field;
Never did Christmas such a harvest yield.

187 (IV. xlvii)

See in burnt colour Phaethon's* device;
Poor fellow! Was it fair to burn him twice?

* He was burnt in attempting to drive the chariot of the sun.

188 (IV. xlix)

A DEFENCE OF EPIGRAM

What makes an epigram he knows not best
Who deems it, Flaccus, but an idle jest.
They rather jest, who Tereus' crime indict
Or the foul banquet of Thyestes write,
Or Icarus equipped with waxen wing
Or Polyphemus and his shepherding.
No fustian ornaments my page abuse
Nor struts in senseless pomp my tragic Muse.
"Men praise," you say, "and call such verse divine."
Yes, they may praise it, but they study mine.

189 (IV. li)

Caecilianus, in the days before you
Six thousand* had, six lads in litter bore you.
Chance has been kind, your pockets overflow,
You have two million†, yet on foot you go.
How recompense such worth? What gift implore?
The litter of past days, ye gods, restore.

* Say £50.   † £16,000, twice a senator's income.

190 (IV. liii)

> That wretch who meets you by the temple gate
> We to our Lady Pallas built of late,
> With staff and scrip, scant hairs all stiff and hoar
> And beard that trails upon the dusty floor,
> Who for his clammy cloak a blanket wears
> And barks for morsels on the crowded stairs,
> To call him Cynic there's no proper ground,
> He's more than hound-like, Cosmus, he's a hound.

191 (IV. liv)

> Collinus, crowned with oak-leaves fair
> With well-earned garlands in your hair,
> Live all your days, if you are wise,
> As if no morrow's sun would rise.
> No man can move the Fates, my friend;
> Strictly to business they attend.
> Join Melior's grace with Crispus' store,
> In spirit Thrasea's self outsoar,
> One sister still unrolls your thread,
> Another slits and you are dead.

192 (IV. lv)

> Lucius, our age's boast, who durst compare
> Tagus and Gaius with Arpinum* rare,
> Let poets born amid the Grecian cities
> Put Thebes and rich Mycenae in their ditties,
> Or shimmering Rhodes or Lacedaemon, school
> Of men not manners, Leda's valley cool.

> * Cicero's birthplace; the other names are of places in Spain,
> the home of Martial.

Be mine to sing in unforgotten lays
Of uncouth Celt and Spanish names the praise.
For ruthless steel Platea and Bilbilis
Far-famed, outmatching German craft, I wis;
Platea engirt with slender restless tide
By Salo, temperer of armour tried;
The song and dance of merry Rixamae
And jocund feasts of our loved Carduae;
Peterus embowered with the blushing rose
And Rigae famed for old ancestral shows.
Our own Silaï skilled light darts to shake,
Turgontus' pool and old Perusia's lake,
And Vetonissa's scanty limpid flow
And the oak woods of hallowed Burado,
Whose lovesome charm the traveller oft beguiles,
Where Manlius' home by Vativesca smiles,
Tilled by stout steers along its winding hill,
A rustic scene, but one that charms me still.
The names may move your laughter to rehearse;
Lucius, they're pretty bad, Bututni's* worse.

* A place in Italy.

193 (IV. lvii)
FAREWELL TO BAIAE

I linger on the wanton Lucrine shore,
Warm grottoes with rock fountains bubbling o'er;
Faustinus, you at Tibur make your home,
Where the tenth milestone marks your steps from Rome.
But the fierce Nemean monarch's* all ablaze
And Baiae swelters in the lion's rays.

* The constellation Leo.

So, sacred founts, sweet shore, farewell to you,
Home of the Nymphs and Naiads all, adieu!
In winter softer far than Tibur's fell,
Your summer drives me to its shades. Farewell!

194 (IV. lix)

A viper through the weeping amber strayed;
The oozy drop its prey the intruder made.
He fretted in the meshes with disgust,
But soon froze stark and stiff within the crust.
Boast, Cleopatra, of thy royal dome;
The worm*, thy rival, finds a nobler tomb.

* The asp that killed Cleopatra.

195 (IV. lx)

To Ardea and Castrum let us go
In the dog-days when all the heaven's aglow.
Tibur's a death trap; Curiatius died,
Sent mid its breezes to the Stygian tide.
Death ranges at his will; when so inclined
In Tibur's bosom he'll Sardinia* find.

* Notoriously unhealthy.

196 (IV. lxi)

Mancinus, you were boasting without end
You had acquired two hundred* from a friend
When we were chatting some four days ago,
'Twas in the poet's lounge, you said you'ld show
Mantles that cost ten thousand† if not more;
They were Pompulla's gift, or so you swore;

* 200,000 sesterces: £1600.   † £80.

From Caelia and from Bassa rubies brave,
True sardonyx, and pearls like ocean-wave.
Last night—'twas during Polio's song—you said
"I'm left six hundred thousand*," as you fled;
At morn a hundred and at noon the same.
"Do you complain of us?" old friends exclaim.
"Silence, for shame then! Or, if that's too dear,
Tell us at last something we like to hear."

* £4800.

197 (IV. lxiii)

From Baulae bound for Baiae, woe is me,
Caerellia perished in the maddened sea.
Ah! cruel waves, forget the glorious time
When you disdained to aid a Nero's crime*.

* Referring to Nero's attempt to drown his mother.

198 (IV. lxiv)

Fair the Hesperian gardens, fairer still
Is Martial's* plot on the Janiculan hill.
An upland level spread along the height,
It basks and gleams in a serener light.
When all the winding vales are masked in cloud,
With a peculiar lustre 'tis endowed.
Gently uprising to the starry sky
His mansion rears its fairy tracery.
Hence you can see seven hills that fence us round
And prize the imperial city to a pound,
High Tusculum and Alba's hill descry,
And every cool retreat that rises nigh;

* His cousin.

Fidenae old and lovely Rubrae's shore,
And Anna's* orchard moist with maiden gore.
You will not hear the loud-voiced boatswain call,
Or hoarse companion of the tow-path bawl.
The broad Flaminian or Salarian show
Where silent wheels of travellers come and go
Nor break your rest, though Mulvian bridge be nigh
Where down the sacred Tiber barges ply.
Town house or country, this its lord commends,
It is his own; 'tis open to his friends.
The open hand, the liberal soul you'll find,
A hospitable hearth, a welcome kind.
You'ld think you saw Alcinous' garden fair
Or newly rich Molorchus† sojourned there.
Ye, who weigh all things in a vulgar scale,
Break with a hundred hoes fair Tibur's vale,
Turn with your plough Praeneste's hanging hill
And Setia with one tenant farmer fill;
Better by far, may I the case decide,
Is Martial's plot than all these acres wide.

* Anna Perenna, to whom human sacrifices were once offered.
† The shepherd who entertained Hercules.

199 (IV. lxvi)

A country dweller, Linus, from your birth,
You know that it's the cheapest life on earth.
Rarely on holidays your coat sees air,
One dinner suit is full ten summers' wear.
Your forest boar, your meadows hare will send,
The wood fat fieldfares your repast to mend.
The fish cry "Come and eat me," in their bed;
A home-made cask supplies a vintage red.

No dainty Grecian page attends your call,
But unkempt home-bred servants throng your hall.
Nor fire nor dogstar devastates your home,
No ship of yours is sunk or rides the foam.
No dice alluring tempt you to a fall;
Nuts are the stakes, if stakes you have at all.
Where is your mother's million cool or more?
Nowhere! You've done what no man did before.

200 (IV. lxvii)

Poor Gaurus asked his Praetor once to lend
A hundred thousand* to an ancient friend.
Said he, "Add but this little to my hoard,
A full-blown knight I can extol my lord."
But he, "I wish I were not more in debt
Than that, to Scorpus, Thallus, and the 'vet.'"
Ungrateful money-bags, your shame endorse:
You grudge the rider and endow the horse.

* £800, a quarter of a knight's income.

201 (IV. lxviii)

TO ONE WHO SERVED HIS GUESTS UNFAIRLY

You dine from the manger and I from the trough;
Then what did you ask me for? Just to show off?

202 (IV. lxix)

Your butler prates of Setine and of Massic,
But scandal gives it titles not so classic.
"Four wives it's cost you*." Gossip's never true,
But I'm not thirsty—much obliged to you.

* Implying that he poisoned them with it.

203 (IV. lxx)

To Ammianus, heir, sole heir, in hope,
His dying father left a rusty rope.
Now, Marcellinus, did it seem to you
That he his sire's decease would ever rue?

204 (IV. lxxii)

You ask me, Quintus, for my little book.
I haven't one. To Tryphon's counter look.
"Pay for your silly stuff and nonsense? Buy?
I won't be such an idiot." Nor will I.

205 (IV. lxxiii)

Youthful Vestinus felt his life was o'er,
His passage booked for the Elysian shore,
And begged the three weird sisters brief delay
To linger out his fast declining day.
Dead to himself, alive to those he loved,
His pious prayers their rugged bosoms moved.
He used the grace, parted his worldly store
And felt indeed a veteran of fourscore.

206 (IV. lxxv)

Blest to your home, Nigrina, blest in life,
Most gracious lady, pattern Roman wife,
A partner's faith you join to marriage vow
And with your heritage your lord endow.
Evadne perished on her husband's pyre,
Alcestis' everlasting name stands higher.
You did far better; you in life were true;
No bed of death to test your honour's due.

207 (IV. lxxvii)

I never asked the gods for luxury,
Contented with my humble poverty.
Beggary, forgive, good-bye! And welcome, pelf!
Strange prayer! I would see Zoilus* hang himself.

* Ep. 73.

208 (IV. lxxviii)

Afer, although you've reached your full three-score,
Your head with many a streak of silver hoar,
You stroll about the town and there's no chair
That does not echo with your greeting fair
No tribune may of your neglect complain
And either consul finds you in his train.
Ten times a day you scale Palatium's hill,
"Sigerus" and "Parthenius"* babbling still.
These tasks are for the young. Poor pantaloon,
There's nothing uglier than an old buffoon.

* Names of courtiers.

209 (IV. lxxix)

At my villa, dear Matho, your face was well known;
You bought it; I cheated; I sold you your own.

210 (IV. lxxxii)

Give Venuleius this my little rhyme,
Rufus, a plaything for his leisure time.
Forgetful of his cares and worries dear
Ask him to read it with indulgent ear;
Not with the first nor with the final cup,
But when the mid feast takes the challenge up.
If it's too much, then fold the leaf in two;
Divided, you may shift to read it through.

211 (IV. lxxxv)

PATRON AND CLIENTS
Compare Ep. 201.

> We drink from glass; your agate cup's a mask
> To hide the secret of your private flask.

212 (IV. lxxxvi)

> Would you commend yourself to ears polite,
> Give heed, my book, and do as I indite.
> Go to Apollinaris, he you'll find
> Is wise and learned but he's fair and kind.
> By him admired and quoted, do not look
> For spiteful snorts, nor fear to serve the cook;
> You'll make no Nessus' shirt for mackerel.
> If he condemns you, you may just as well
> Run to salt-merchants' stalls, a sorry hack,
> And let the boys scrawl copies on your back.

213 (IV. lxxxviii)

> Christmas* is past. My humble offering,
> A squandered thought, no answering gift did bring.
> No mangled drachm of silver was my dole,
> Or napkin sent as grumbling client's toll†,
> No Gallic tunny in a ruddy jar
> Nor baby figs have reached me from afar,
> No rough Picentine fruit in basket small
> To show you had remembered me at all.
> With smiles and catchwords you the world may flout;
> They're thrown away on me; I've found you out.

* The Saturnalia, much resembling our Christmas.
† For clients' presents to patrons, see Ep. 186.

214 (IV. lxxxix)

We've filled the scroll; "Hold, hold, enough!" I say,
But still you want to plod your inky way.
Heigho! 'tis finis, and the gap to fill
One page was plenty, yet you're restless still.
The reader flags and grumbles at the stuff,
And now the very penman cries "Enough."

215 (V. i)

Whether on Alba's hills thou chance to be
Beholding Trivia here, and there the sea,
Or the weird sisters hearken your replies
Where the suburban flood outspreading lies,
If old Caieta please or sungod's daughter*,
Or Anxur glittering with its healthful water,
This book, protector of the world, receive
Whose welfare bids us in the gods believe.
Only accept, I'll take the thing for read,
An easy dupe with swollen Gallic head.

* Circe for Circeii.

216 (V. v)

TO DOMITIAN'S LIBRARIAN

Custodian eloquent of learning's shrine,
Sextus, new registrar of words divine,
To you cur lord confides each dawning care,
And in his inmost thoughts you have a share.
Give me a niche and corner to abide
By Pedo, Marsus and Catullus' side.
By the great epic of the war for Rome*
You'll find a shrine for Virgil's stately tome.

* The emperor's poem.

217 (V. vi)

If not displeasing or unworth the care,
To your Parthenius*, Muses, make my prayer.
"So be your age in Caesar's welfare blest
And envy leave your happy hours at rest,
So Burrus† image you, my shrinking page
Bring to the portals of a holier age‡.
You know the seasons of our sovereign's grace,
When smiling with his own familiar face,
Denying nought. Fear no ill-timed petition;
Not with loud querulous plea desires admission
With blackened stick this cedar-scented scroll.
Don't thrust it out, just hold the purple roll
As if 'twere nought. I know our Muses' lord;
He'll ask the dainty of his own accord."

* Chamberlain of Domitian.
† Son of the above.
‡ Domitian made himself censor, perhaps honestly though absurdly.

218 (V. vii)

Once in a thousand years the Assyrian bird*
Rose from its ashes, so the bards averred.
So Rome† her ancient slough of age doth mew
And, like her sovereign, youthful looks endue.
Vulcan, forgive your quarrel, I entreat;
Though Mars our sire, our mother's Venus sweet.
So may your consort, I devoutly beg,
Forget those chains and nurse your limping leg.

* The phoenix.
† Much defaced by the civil wars and now restored.

219 (V. viii)

A SHAM KNIGHT

"The edict of our sovereign master's grace,
Whereby our knighthood keeps its ancient place*
At play or pageant, sure of clowns' removal,
Is safe," said Phasis, "from our disapproval"
(Phasis with purple mantles all aglow);
"Now we can sit more comfortably so;
At last our order's to its rights restored;
No crush, no pushing by the vulgar horde."
While he reclined, discoursing in such wise,
An officer desired my lord to rise.

* The first fourteen rows at the theatre were set apart for the knights.

220 (V. ix)

I was ailing last winter and sent through the snow
For Mackenzie, who hastened with Fisher and Co.
Oh! the frost and their fingers! Heaven plague you,
    Mackenzie;
I've now what I hadn't before—influenzie.

221 (V. x)

In his own age no poet's known;
Men like all ages but their own.
Not to the dead their praise they're giving;
'Tis only that they hate the living.
So Pompey's ugly walk we love,
And Catulus' old-fashioned Jove.
In Virgil's time 'twas "Ennius sage";
Homer was laughed at in his age.
Menander played to empty benches
And none read Ovid but his wenches.

Pray, my impatient Muse, don't worry.
If death's due first, I'm in no hurry.

222 (v. xi)

A FASHIONABLE PLEADER

Sardonyx, emerald, diamond, jasper rare
Each movement of my Stella's finger share.
Though they be many, yet his Muse has more;
These are but trinkets from a fairy store.

223 (v. xii)

The same.

If Masthlion's brow uprears a tottering weight
Upon a pole, if children seven or eight
Ninus with all his mighty sinews bears,
'Tis no hard matter, this exploit of theirs.
Why, on one finger joint, beyond a doubt,
Stella a dozen maids* will bear about.

* *I.e.*, their portraits on rings.

224 (v. xiii)

Callistratus, I am, as always, poor;
That's not to say a man unknown, obscure.
I'm read the wide world through; "That's he," men say,
And what death gives to few is mine to-day.
Your roof-beams on a hundred pillars rest,
A freedman's fortune rattles in your chest,
Vast tracts of Egypt your enclosure blocks
And Parma shears for you her countless flocks
The contrast mark. I'm what you cannot be,
The meanest man can match your luxury.

225 (V. xiv)

See note on Ep. 219.

Nanneius, that old stager, wont to sit
In happier days file-leader of the pit,
His quarters thrice beat up, thrice shifted ground;
Now between seats an awkward third he's found.
Wrapped in a hood he pries and peers about
And with one ugly eye surveys the rout.
Bombed out again, the gangway's his retreat,
Where he ill-poised on knee and endmost seat
Sitting or standing varies at caprice,
And snubs in turn the knights and the police.

226 (V. xvi)

I might write Epics; that a humbler fame
Contents me, reader, I have you to blame.
You read and quote them both to high and low,
But what it costs to me you hardly know.
If I were minded in the courts to plead
And lend my aid to prisoners in their need,
To me would journey many a flask of Spain
And many a copper coin my bosom stain*.
But they who carol me at feast and rout
Dismiss me with a thank-you—or without.
The classic poets sought not praise but pence;
Alexis brought his bard a competence.
"Bravo!" you cry, "we're vastly in your debt."
You hypocrite! you'll turn me lawyer yet.

* For presents to patrons, see Ep. 186.

227 (v. xvii)

Gellia, who boasted of your ancient line,
Despising knighthood as too base decline,
And nothing prized beneath a laticlave*,
Whom have you after all? A porter knave†.

* A knight of the higher class, from the broad stripe he wore.
† A play on some religious title.

228 (v. xviii)

At Christmas* time, when kerchiefs fly around,
Spoons, tablets, paper, in my house are found,
And heaps of mouldy damsons in their cone;
I sent you verse and homebred verse alone.
Perchance you think me greedy and unkind;
Insidious presents are not to my mind.
Gifts are like hooks; the greedy wrasse is shy,
But falls a victim to the dangled fly.
The poor man nothing, Quintianus, spends,
If he's a gentleman, on wealthy friends.

* Ep. 213.

229 (v. xix)

If truth be told, great Caesar, then your age
Outrivals all the best on history's page.
When were our shores graced with such well-earned bays?
When did the Palatine win louder praise?
When was our Rome so fair and great to see?
What other time basked in such liberty?
But we lay one great blemish at its door;
Never were friends less generous to the poor.
Who showers his gifts upon a trusty friend?
When does a knight only for love attend?

To send a half-pound spoon as Christmas fee
Or half-crown coat is prodigality.
Our purse-proud patrons praise this bounty mean;
Who prate of gold are "few and far between."
Since all men fail, Caesar, to you I turn;
No greater laurels could a sovereign earn.
I see you smile with an indulgent wink;
This counsel's for myself, not you, I think.

230 (V. xx)

TO HIS COUSIN

Were I with you, dear Martial, then be sure
That we would bask in sunny days secure.
If we could while our lazy hours away
And live the simple life from day to day,
We'ld shun the wealthy hall, the dismal court,
Nor to our patronizing friends resort,
But walks and talks and books and cloisters cool
And baths and riding and Agrippa's pool,
These were our haunts, these pastimes would enthrall;
Now neither of us truly lives at all.
Suns rise and set and swell the reckoning. Say,
Does life mean anything? Then live to-day.

231 (V. xxii)

THE MORNING CALL

I long to see you and have earned the right,
So do not think I want to lose you quite.
But then I live by Tiber's pier, you know,
Where rustic Flora sees old Jove below.

So I must toil up the Suburran steep
And scale the slippery steps through refuse deep.
Scarce through the mule-teams can I force my way
And massive marble hoisted on a dray.
To make things worse, when all that way I've come,
The porter tells me you are not at home.
This the reward my toil and sweating win?
'Twas scarce worth while, if I should find you in.
Forward politeness courts discourtesy.
Till you sleep later, you're no lord for me.

232 (V. xxiii)

Bassus, in orange mantles you were clad
Before the theatre reforms*, my lad;
Now our kind censor's care has changed it all
And knights in comfort hear the marshal's call,
You go in purple or in red attire
And hope to prove even truth itself a liar.
Four hundred thousand† none for clothing pay,
Else my friend Cordus‡ were a knight to-day.

* See Ep. 219.   † £3200,—a knight's income.
† Ep. 235. Cordus, though well dressed, was not a knight.

233 (V. xxiv)

ON A FAVOURITE GLADIATOR

Hermes, gallant darling of our day,
Hermes, versed in every weapon's way,
Hermes, organizing or obeying,
Hermes, guard-room tumbling and dismaying,
Who but Hermes can turn Helius blue?
Who but Hermes Advolans undo?

Hermes, merciful to vanquished foes,
Hermes, who no understudy knows,
Hermes, whose contractor wealth amasses,
Hermes, joy and smart of barrack lasses,
Hermes, or in Mars' or Neptune's guise, or*
Hermes, dangerous with drooping visor,
Hermes, miracle of record-breaking,
Hermes, past comparing or mistaking!

* *I.e.*, either fully armed, or with net and trident.

234 (V. XXV)
A KNIGHT IN ALL BUT FORTUNE
See Ep. 219.

Where is your fortune? Here you may not bide;
The marshal's coming; quick, fly hence and hide.
Someone recall him from his painful way;
Some open coffer-lid his lack defray.
What name shall I record for all to hear?
He must not pass unhonoured to his bier.
Would'st rather drench the stage with ruddy shower,
Quaff the moist fragrance of a saffron bower,
Enrich a race-horse, to your favours cold,
That men may see his jockey's nose in gold?
O rich in vain! Fie, friendship light as air!
You read and praise; oh what a chance is there!

235 (V. XXVI)

I called you "arbiter of outdoor grace"—
'Twas folly, Cordus*, and I've lost the place.
But, if the epithet still rankles deep,
Call me an ass who dresses like a sheep.

* Ep. 91.

236 (v. xxix)

> In sending a hare to me, Gellia, you say
> "You'll be handsome, dear Marcus, a week from to-day!"
> If you say so in earnest, my dear, by the look of it
> I wish I may die if you ever partook of it.

237 (v. xxx)

> Varro, unrivalled in the tragic strain,
> Nor less without a peer in lyric vein,
> Put off your work, let not Catullus' mime
> Or dainty elegiac waste your time,
> But through the smoke of mad December read
> A verse appropriate to the season's need,
> Unless it seems to you less grievous loss
> To spend your Christmas time at pitch and toss

238 (v. xxxi)

> See how the lads affront the meek-eyed steers
> And how the bull his living freight uprears,
> To one his horns, to one his withers lends,
> One o'er the ponderous beast his spear extends:
> Rage turns to steadfast rock; less firm their stand
> Upon the level plain or shifting sand:
> They feel no fear; assured of victory
> The children mock the bull's anxiety

239 (v. xxxii)

> Dead Crispus to his wife left little store;
> Of course: he'd spent it on himself before.

240 (V. xxxiv)

Flaccilla, Fronto, take her as I write,
My precious darling and my soul's delight,
Let not Erotion fear the shades around
And the fell jaws of the Tartarean hound*.
Had she but lived till six more days were told,
She had survived six winters and their cold.
There let her play amidst our fellowship
And lisp my name with dainty stammering lip.
Her gentle head, Earth, with soft mosses dress,
And as her footstep light be thy caress.

* Cerberus.

241 (V. xxxv)

Euclides, clad in scarlet, loves to boast
Two hundred comes from farms on Patrae's coast,
From Corinth more; from Leda he's descended
And, if the marshal jogs him, he's offended.
A knight he is of title, wealth and fame:
A key* fell from his bosom. What a shame!

* Of his master's cupboard, showing him a slave.

242 (V. xxxvi)

Faustinus, one I praised; if he deny
The debt, more scoundrel he, and more fool I.

243 (V. xxxvii)

Sweeter than swan, dear child, of plumage grey,
Or gentle lambs that by Galaesus play,
More dainty than the shell of Lucrine lake,
That o'er the pearl might well precedence take,

Or than the polished Indian ivory,
Or snow fresh fallen or lily's pageantry,
Or fleece of Spain or Rhenish maiden's hair,
Or golden mice or Paestum's rosebed rare,
Like choicest honey-comb from Attic land
Or ball of amber snatched from maiden's hand;
Compared to her the peacock were not fair,
The squirrel gentle or the phoenix rare.
When scarce six winters of her life had sped
A cruel destiny has shorn her thread;
My love, my darling and my playmate dear!
But Paetus will not have me shed a tear.
Beating his breast, tearing his hair he cries,
"For shame, to weep so when a slave-girl dies.
I buried my own treasure, my dear wife,
Proud, noble, wealthy, yet endure my life!"
O noble Paetus, what an iron will!
Some twenty millions, and he's living still.

244 (V. xxxviii)

For the law of the theatre, see Ep. 219 note.

A knight's estate* has Calliodorus. True:
But look you; Fuscus, he's a brother too.
To split a cherry were a wiser course
Than halve this sum. Two men can't ride one horse.
Hang your intruding brother, out, I say!
You were a Castor†, if he cleared the way.
Sound logic, Calliodorus, it defeats
To say you're one, and occupy two seats.
You can't sit with your brother, when all's done.
Then sit like Leda's children, one by one.

* Ep. 232.
† For the story, compare Ep. 19. Castor however sacrificed himself only.

245 (V. xxxix)

Some thirty times a year you make your will;
I send you dripping thymy sweet-meats still.·
Charinus, pardon: I'm against the wall;
Make wills less frequently, or once for all
Fulfil the pledge of that elusive cough;
My wallet and my purse are dry; be off.
Had you his humble crust as often shared
Old Croesus now with Irus* had compared.

* A beggar in Homer.

246 (V. xl)

TOO MANY IRONS IN THE FIRE

Venus you paint, and to Minerva pray:
Small wonder that your works "gang aft agley."

247 (V. xlii)

Some cunning burglar will abstract your plate,
A godless fire your roof will devastate,
A debtor steal both interest and loan,
A barren field will turn your seed to stone.
A wily wench will strip your steward bare,
The greedy sea engulf your galleon's ware.
Give to a friend and fortune is checkmated;
Such wealth will ever as your own be rated.

248 (V. xlix)

I saw you sitting there and thought you three,—
Your scalp's triplicity perplexing me.
Lovelocks adorn you, few and far between,
Such as might well betoken sweet seventeen

Your noddle's bare and in the desert rude
No single hair affronts the solitude.
This blunder paid you well at Christmas last
When our good sovereign helped to break your fast.
Laden with three bread-baskets you returned;
Even such was Geryon* as I have learned.
Avoid Philippus' porch, I beg, my friend;
If Hercules† behold you, there's an end.

* A three-headed giant slain by Hercules.
† *I.e.*, his statue there.

249 (v. l)

If you're not asked to dinner any day,
You're up in arms and spoiling for a fray.
Fain, Charopinus, would you run me through,
If e'er my hearthstone has no place for you.
May I not snatch one morsel in repose?
Such greediness beyond all conscience goes.
Don't poke your snout in every pot and pan,
But leave my kitchen to itself, my man.

250 (v. li)

A LEARNED HERMIT

The fellow whom you see brief-laden, stand,
Engirt with notary-boys on either hand,
Frowning on marshalled papers, legal fetters,
And tabulated files of ancient letters,
The spit of Brutus, Cato, Cicero,
Torture will not compel him to say "bo!"
He can't give Latin greeting, no nor Greek.
You doubt me? Say "good day" and make him speak.

251 (v. lii)

Grateful for all your gifts I still shall be;
"Why then be silent?" Well, you speak for me.
If to a friend your kindness I report,
With, "Yes, he told me so" he cuts me short.
Some tasks are not so suitable for two,
So thank you, Postumus, I'll wait for you.
Believe me, gifts, however rich they be,
Lose all their value by loquacity.

252 (v. liii)

Why sing Medea or Thyestes' stew?
What's Niobe, Andromache, to you?
Bassus, the theme most fitted for your lyre
Is he who felt the flood or scorching fire*.

* Deucalion or Phaethon. His poems deserve one or the other fate.

253 (v. liv)

THE FOREIGN PROFESSOR OF RHETORIC

Our orator has got our names by rote;
He said "How are you, Cholmondeley?" without note.

254 (v. lvi)

What teacher shall instruct your son and heir?
This is your study and your haunting care.
Virgil and Cicero alike eschew;
Dispense with rhetoric and grammar too;
Leave great Tutilius* to be talked about;
If son of yours turn poet, turn him out.

* An advocate.

Suppose he wants a money-grubbing trade,
Have him a harper or a flute-player made.
Has he no brains? A suitable career
He'll find as builder or as auctioneer.

255 (v. lviii)

You'll live to-morrow, Postumus, you cry.
When will this morrow, pray, be passing by?
How far is it? Where shall we seek it, where?
In Parthia or Armenia is its lair?
To-morrow's old as Priam, Nestor. Why,
What is the price that can to-morrow buy?
You'll live to-morrow? Now's too late, I say.
He's wise, my Postumus, who lived yesterday.

256 (v. lx)

Although you sneer and snarl and show your teeth,
I'll no perpetual bay to you bequeath.
Fain would you have your questionable name
Read through the world and earn a stolen fame.
Why need you leave a mark? 'Tis sad, I own,
But 'tis your destiny to die unknown.
Who love the task your currish hide may baste,
To foul my claws with carrion I've no taste.

257 (v. lxii)

Pray walk into my garden; 'tis your right,
If you can lie on churlish turf all night.
My furniture all further call refuses
And every guest must bring the stuff he uses.

Uncushioned couches, battered and forlorn,
Their mouldering straps lament and hangings torn.
Let's share the burden; I've the ground provided,
You furnish; still, that's doing less than I did.

258 (v. lxiii)

"Marcus, I say, what think you of my book?"
Thus, Ponticus, you cry with anxious look.
Splendid, magnificent; 'tis perfect quite;
Regulus' self to you must yield his right.
"You mean it? Jove and Caesar prosper you!"
I'm sure he's very welcome—if I do.

* Ep. 100.

259 (v. lxiv)

Callistus, pour two bumpers, pour them neat;
Melt, Alcimus, the snow to quench their heat.
In oozy spikenard steep your perfumed hair
And bow my head with rosy garlands fair.
From yonder Mausoleum* breathes the sigh,
"Live while thou mayest, gods themselves must die."

* Of Augustus, Ep. 93.

260 (v. lxv)

Lion and boar won Hercules admission
To heaven, in spite of Juno's opposition;
With them Antaeus, thrown on Libyan strand,
Fell Eryx, with Sicilian gauntlet tanned,
And Cacus, forest tyrant, to whose door
Came oxen by his cunning tail-before.

By Caesar's wonders set how small are these!
Each rising morn far greater battles sees.
What far more monstrous lions perish here,
What huger boars are spitted by your spear!
Could three-fold Geryon* come and fight again,
You've one to beat the shepherd hind of Spain.
Let Hydra boast his hundred heads immense,
The Egyptian beasts could shame his proud pretence.
To Alcides for his service soon was given
A home above; may you not yet win heaven.

* See above 248.

261 (v. lxvi)

I give you greeting, but get none from you,
Pontilianus. So a long adieu.

262 (v. lxvii)

When swallows southward winged their airy way,
One bird was tempted in the nest to stay.
Northward in spring high soaring through the blue
They learnt the treason and the traitor slew.
Full vengeance then was theirs, though late in time,
For Itys' murder* and the mother's crime.

* In the legend Procne murdered her child and was turned into a swallow.

263 (v. lxix)

ON THE MURDER OF CICERO BY ANTONY

Mark Antony, rival of Egypt's blame*,
Whose very death-roll blanched at Tully's name,
What madness bares thy sword on Roman strand?
A very Catiline such guilt had bann'd.

* The murder of Pompey.

What treasure on a graceless soldier spent
To rid thee of that old man eloquent!
And could those treasures purchase silence? No,
To-day all tongues will tell of Cicero.

264 (v. lxx)

Ten millions had Syriscus for his dole;
Bookshops and baths accounted for the whole.
What gluttony, to lap ten million up,
For ever feast, and never pass the cup!

265 (v. lxxi)

IN THE SABINE HILLS

Where Trebula on valleys cool looks down
And fields are verdant in the dog-days brown,
Lands where the Lion's glare can ne'er intrude,
A happy valley by the west wind wooed;
Faustinus, there's your autumn's cool retreat;
'Twill be a winter Tibur in the heat.

266 (v. lxxiv)

The East and West yield Pompey's children graves:
His home is Libya or the salt sea waves:
Three continents must fence such ruins round.
This wreck could not be gathered in one mound.

267 (v. lxxvi)

As Mithradates, drinking poison still,
Came to be proof against the deadly ill,
You too have learnt by supping for a groat
How to subsist upon a single oat.

268 (v. lxxvii)

A GOOD LISTENER

> Marullus, 'twas prettily said, as I hear,
> That you never go out without oil in your ear.

269 (v. lxxviii)

> If solitary dinners give you fits,
> Come dine with me, you shall have choice tit-bits;
> Cheap lettuces and leeks and tunny fish
> Garnished with eggs, o'erspreading all the dish;
> On a dark platter there a cabbage green
> All hot to scorch your fingers will be seen;
> A sausage on a hasty-pudding placed,
> Pale beans and bacon's appetizing taste.
> For your dessert some withered grapes I'll bring
> And pears to Syrian titles answering,
> Chestnuts from Naples, roast by scorching glow;
> My wine's not good; drinking will make it so.
> If Bacchus makes you hungry, there will be
> Olives fresh plucked from a Picenian tree.
> Hot pease and lupine will complete our diet;
> A humble catalogue, I'll not deny it.
> You'll tell no lies nor hear them, only smile;
> No host will read a ponderous tome the while.
> The humble pipe will tune a simple lay,
> Not dull or boisterous but alert and gay.
> Such is my supper. Claudia you prefer,
> Claudia's coming, you will follow her.

270 (v. lxxix)

> Twelve times but one from supper you withdrew,
> Twelve times but one your clothing must renew,

Lest haply moisture in its warmth might lurk
And draught to open pores a mischief work.
I dine with you, yet is my raiment dry;
A single suit is airy in July.

271 (v. lxxx)

If you a fraction of an hour can spare,
Severus, lend it to my earnest prayer.
I want your critic's eye. 'Tis hard, you say,
To bear the loss and waste a holiday.
Could you by chance, forgive my boldness, fee
Secundus* as *amicus curiae*?
My little book will owe much more to you
Than to its master, if you read it through.
He'll face the world at ease, escaping thus
The restless stone of weary Sisyphus†.
When once it's passed your scrutinizing eye
And wise Secundus' file, 'twill all defy.

* Perhaps Pliny.
† Who rolled the stone nearly to the top of the hill when it fell back.

272 (v. lxxxiv)

Now the whining lad his nuts forsakes,
    Rated back to lessons by the Doctor.
Beery lads, whom Bulldog* dicing takes
From the rattling tavern's ale and cakes,
    Cry Peccavi to the Senior Proctor.
Christmas goes and yet no presents greet me,
    Great or smaller, faithless lady mine,
Christmas goes; Ethel, you think to cheat me.
Saints' days come; Ethel, you won't defeat me.
    Take your present for my Valentine.

* Here for the attendant of the Aedile.

273 (VI. i)

Dear Martial*, best friend,
My sixth book I send
    Beseeching your critical ear;
And then it will dare
Without worry or care
    Before Caesar himself to appear.

* His cousin.

274 (VI. iii)

A NEW-BORN SON OF DOMITIAN

Come forth, true scion of the promised line,
Own son of Mars; shine out, great infant, shine!
Some day to you the eternal reins will fall,
Old son of older father, ruling all.
Gold threads of life for you shall Julia* pull,
And interweave the web with Phrixus'† wool.

* A niece of Domitian.
† He who rode on the ram with the golden fleece.

275 (VI. v)

I bought a farm; it cost me quite a plum;
Lend me a hundred thousand. What, you're dumb,
Caecilianus? "As a loan you ask it?"
Precisely. I'll return the empty basket.

276 (VI. vi)

There are three actors. Not enough for some, eh?
Paula loves four, Lupercus. One's a dummy*.

* The laws of the drama allowed a fourth actor if he did not speak.

277 (VI. viii)

A certain shrewd hunks had a certain fair daughter;
Four captains, five authors, six barristers sought her;
To none of all them would Papa lend an ear
But at once gave her hand to a glib auctioneer.
If professions by cash, not by credit, are tried,
Who shall say that old Squaretoes chose ill for the bride?

278 (VI. ix)

IN THE WRONG SEAT

See Ep. 219.

In Pompey's theatre sleep overtakes you.
D'you mind, Lupercus, if the tip-staff wakes you?

279 (VI. x)

I asked of Jupiter some thousands few:
"He'll give," he said, "who gave me temples new*."
Temples he gave to Jove but nought to me.
Oh! small request! Alas! my modesty.
But yet how sweetly with no look unkind
He read the meek petition that I signed.
With such a smile full many a Dacian crown
He gave, to the Capitol driving up and down.
Tell me, dear Maid†, if he, refusing, smile,
When he assents, how will he laugh the while.
Thus I; then she, her Gorgon laid aside,
"Fool, what's not granted yet is not denied."

* Domitian.
† Minerva, Domitian's favourite goddess.

280 (VI. xi)

Pylades and Orestes are no more;
You wonder, Marcus. 'Twas not so of yore;
One roll, one dainty fieldfare served the pair,
'Twixt friend and friend it still was share and share.
You guzzle oysters, I eat whelks alone,
And yet my stomach's Roman like your own.
You go in purple, I in wool appear;
How can a cobbler love a grand vizier?
Where's the Orestes for my Pylades?
Love I'll return, but spare your courtesies.

281 (VI. xiii)

ON A STATUE OF DOMITIAN'S NIECE AS VENUS ACCOMPANIED
BY A CUPID

Who, lovely Julia, fashioned thee so fair?
Was it Athene's, or her sculptor's care?
The snow-white marble effigy, at strife
With pulsing nature, would outdo the life.
See Venus gently with her cestus toy,
Rapt from the shoulders of the Idalian boy*.
To bring their gadding lords to bow the knee
Venus and Juno will appeal to thee.

* Cupid who had stolen it.

282 (VI. xiv)

TO ONE WHO ABSTAINED FROM WRITING

You can write decent verses, so you say,
Laberius. Well, why don't you, any way?
Who will not make good verses when he might,
He is a man, Laberius; yes, you're right.

283 (VI. xv)

An ant was loitering in the amber shade;
The oozy drop the beast a prisoner made.
So what in life had been a worthless thing
Has now grown precious in its burying.

284 (VI. xvii)

Cinnamus, barber, Cinna's name you fake;
A barbarous clipping that, and no mistake.
So, if your name were really Robert, we
Should see it turned to Robber presently.

285 (VI. xviii)

In Spanish earth my Saloninus lies;
No nobler soul o'er Stygian waters plies.
We may not weep; Priscus is left behind,
His better part, and therefore he's resigned.

286 (VI. xix)

This is no case of murder or assault,
Or poison. My three kids comprise your fault.
I say my neighbour's stolen them away;
"Well, prove your case," the upright judge will say.
You rant of Cannae and the Pontic shore
And falsehood of the Punic conqueror.
Of Sulla, Marius, Mucius you protest:
Well, my three kids now: never mind the rest.

287 (VI. xxiv)

Charisianus is a gay young dog, a
Mere fop; he goes at Christmas* in a tŏga.

* Ep. 213.

7–2

288 (VI. xxvii)

Nepos, you're twice my neighbour, for you're found
Near Flora's gate and old Ficeliae's bound*.
Though you've a daughter in whose face appear
Your image and her mother's honour clear,
Spare not too much your vintage old to shed
And rather fill your casks with coins instead.
Good she may be and wealthy; let her drink
New wine. It will grow old with her. I think
A father may enjoy the good he stores;
Old Caecuban is not for bachelors.

* At Rome and in the Sabine hills.

289 (VI. xxviii)

Poor Glaucia, Melior's freedman whom we knew,
His master's chief delight, Rome's bitter rue,
Here lies beside the old Flaminian way;
So modest, innocent, quick-witted, gay;
Not yet thirteen. Here, wayfarer, make moan:
So may you weep no darling of your own.

290 (VI. xxix)

No common slave from greedy dealer's store,
But worth his master's holy love before,
Ere he could feel his patron's bounty free,
Melior gave Glaucia his liberty.
His virtues, beauty earned it. Whom more sweet
Or whom more like Apollo could you meet?
The paragons of youth few summers tell:
If thou love true, pray not to love too well.

291 (VI. XXX)

If on the day you promised me to lend
Six thousand, I had had it then to spend,
I could have owed you fifty times the sum;
The months rolled by, and now at last it's come.
Now must the truth, the very truth, be told?
Paetus, I fear, I fear you've lost your gold.

292 (VI. XXXII)

When civil war was trembling in the scale
And weakling Otho* might perchance prevail,
With such dear price of victory ill content
His steadfast hand his labouring bosom rent.
If Cato Caesar in his life surpassed,
Thou hadst no rival, Otho, at the last.

* Otho, defeated by Vitellius, killed himself to prevent more bloodshed.

293 (VI. XXXV)

Pleading, you shouted loud for an extension;
The umpire smiled, but granted the suspension.
But you, half leaning back with cup to lip,
Sip the warm tide, and prattle as you sip.
Both voice and thirst, Caecilian, satisfy;
Your clock is worked by water; drink it dry.

294 (VI. XXXVIII)

See how young Regulus*, not three years old,
To praise his father when he pleads is bold.
At sight of him, his mother left alone,
He feels his father's laurels are his own.

* Son of the orator of Ep. 100.

The crowd, the judges and the shouting wild
And the full court charm the precocious child.
Thus well-bred foals the race-course will delight
And tender calves with hornless forehead fight.
Gods, to the parents grant their earnest prayer;
May Regulus hear his offspring, she the pair.

295 (VI. xli)

That fellow with the wool about his throat
Says he can't speak. He can't be silent, note.

296 (VI. xlii)

If of Etruscus' baths he's shy,
Unwashed will Oppianus die.
Nowhere's so soft a wave in sooth,
Patavium's founts to maids uncouth,
Soft Sinuessa, Passer spring
So boiling, Anxur, haughty king,
Old Phoebus' baths or Baiae fair.
Nowhere's a purer, calmer air.
The light lags longer, and the day
Glides with a lazier course away.
On Spartan green-stone eyes may feast,
And Afric vies with quarried East.
With droughty heat the onyx shimmers
And serpentine like fire-flake glimmers.
If Spartan rite your wishes meet
You'll choose the clear unmoistened heat,
And, for a plunge, to suit your taste,
There's Marcian spring or Virgin* chaste.

* The aqueduct of Agrippa.

You'ld think there was no water there,
But Lydian marble gleaming bare.
He turns on me a vacant eye.
Unwashed then, Oppianus, die.

297 (VI. xliii)

While happy Baiae pleases you
Who swim its sulphur waters through,
To me Nomentum yields a cote
To rest in, with sufficient plot:
Not Baiae or Lucrine more fair,
Not, Castricus, your treasures rare.
Time was, to fashionable bath
I loved to tread my weary path;
Now a suburban snug recess
Suffices me for idleness.

298 (VI. xlvi)

TURF MORALS

Jockey, you flog your team and make no way;
That's a big business that you do to-day.

299 (VI. xlvii)

Sweet Nymph, that risest under starry dome,
Pellucid fountain of my Stella's home,
Or by Egeria* sent from Dian's shrine,
Or latest lingerer of the Muses Nine†,
My sickness trespassed on thy waters healing;
Accept this virgin pig for my misdealing.
Henceforth contented, let thy favour bring
Health to my thirst, and to my joy no sting.

* Egeria the goddess of Numa's spring near Rome.
† For Stella as poet, see Ep. 640.

300 (VI. li)

Of my wrongs, Lupercus, slighted,
To your table uninvited,
   I'll requite the sum.
Should you bid, entreat, implore me,
Should you kneel in tears before me,
   Hear me swear, I'll—come!

301 (VI. lii)

Here lies entombed, cut off from budding life,
      Pantagathus, his master's love and care;
Skilled, light as butterfly, to ply the knife
      And rid my cheek of its superfluous hair.
Be tender, earth, lie gently on him, sand;
Thou canst not touch more lightly than his hand.

302 (VI. lv)

With cinnamon and cassia dark your hue,
Your perfumes more than nest of phoenix knew,
Laugh, Coracinus, at my lack of scent;
You may; I take it as a compliment.

303 (VI. lvii)

You call in art to fill up nature's void,
      And on your frowsy pate sham lovelocks trace;
For these a barber need not be employed,
      Phoebus; a sponge will better meet the case.

304 (VI. lix)

Baccara frets and fumes at summer weather,
    Of woollen mantles he's such hundreds piled;
He hopes for gloom and storms and snows together
    And blames the winter when the day is mild.
How has my threadbare cloak your rancour earned,
    That falls a victim to the lightest breeze?
Had you economy or mercy learned
    You'ld face the summer out in cloaks of frieze!

305 (VI. lx)

Faustinus, now Pompullus' name is made,
Through the wide world his verses he'll parade.
May flaxen haired Usipi* have such fame
And all that love not the Ausonian name.
"Yet he's a certain knack: he's good enough."
Believe me, fame is made of other stuff.
The moths and cockroaches on talent wait,
And cooks determine wit and learning's fate.
What makes a book immortal, who can tell?
A "touch of nature" must be there as well.

* A German tribe on the Rhine.

306 (VI. lxi)

A HIT

All Rome extols and loves and quotes my lines
    And every bosom holds them, every hand;
See one that reddens, pales, yawns, stares and pines.
    Ah! now at last their worth I understand.

307 (VI. lxii)

Salanus, of his only son bereft,
A prey to fortune-hunting rogues is left.
Pour in your presents, Oppianus, thick;
Some other vulture else will be too quick.

308 (VI. lxiii)

Before your very eyes the snare is set;
Why, Marianus, walk into the net?
Fool, your betrayer in your will to write
And for successor choose a parasite!
"He sent me costly presents ": 'twas his bait.
Pray, does the quarry not the angler hate?
He will not mourn your ashes as he ought.
If you would have him weep, then leave him nought.

309 (VI. lxv)

"You write your epigrams the Epic way."
'Tis common, Tucca; and, besides, one may.
"But they are tedious." Common too, and sound;
And, if you want them, couplets may be found.
Come now, let's enter into partnership;
I've liberty to prose and you to skip.

310 (VI. lxx)

Cotta for sixty years or more, 'tis said,
Has, Marcianus, spent no day in bed.
No Dasius, Alcon, Symmachus he sees *
And snaps his fingers at the doctor's fees.
Let's bring our years to book and count as lost
All that pain, fever, fainting, sickness cost.

* Physicians of the day.

We're really children though our hair be grey.
Who counts as long old Priam's, Nestor's day,
Is much deceived and resting on a reed.
Life is not life, but health is life indeed.

311 (VI. lxxiv)

That man who's dining in the lowest place,
With smudge of oil across a three-haired space,
With mastich boring the expanse beneath,
Lies, Aesculanus, for he has no teeth.

312 (VI. lxxv)

When you dish me a fieldfare or flatcake or thigh
Of a hare or the like for my table's supply,
Saying "Pontia sends her tit-bits for a greeting,"
I can't say I like them, for giving or eating.

313 (VI. lxxvi)

Here Fuscus lies, late Captain of the Guard,
Who for our sovereign kept true watch and ward.
Fortune, I thank thee. His last place of rest
No hostile threat henceforth may e'er molest.
The Dacian neck beneath our yoke is laid;
His spirit dominates the conquered glade.

314 (VI. lxxvii)

Aper, you're poor as Irus* and as strong
As young Parthenopaeus, famed in song:

* A sturdy beggar in Homer.

So stout Artemidorus could not maul you.
Why must you have six sturdy lads to haul you?
Like Atlas* and his mule you're pointed out,
Or the swart monster and his black mahout.
"Why is my litter so offensive?" Hear,
You're dead†, and dead men only want a bier.

* A dwarf.
† Socially a cipher, as a parvenu. Compare Zoilus, Ep. 103, etc.

315 (VI. lxxviii)

The toper Phryx was scant of sight,
His left eye blind, and bleared his right.
The doctor frankly spoke his mind,
"Cease drinking, sir, or go stone blind."
Phryx laughing cried "Farewell my peeper!
Large glasses, ho! I'll drink the deeper."
The luckless issue who can doubt?
The wine went in, the eye went out.

316 (VI. lxxx)

For welcome novelty, the land of Nile
Sent Caesar Christmas roses. With a smile
The sailor passed our suburbs on his way,
"Pharos and Memphis gardens, where are they?
The wealth of spring, the sweets that Flora cheer,
The pride of Paestum's roses, all are here."
He wandered wide and turned his gaze around;
Festoons of roses right and left he found.
Bow, Nile, to Roman winter. If you will,
We'll send you roses, send your harvests still

317 (VI. lxxxii)

A certain fellow once my measure took
    Just as a purchaser or trainer might.
Digging my ribs, with mischief in his look
    He said, "Are you great Martial, famous wight?
Your quirks and cranks are known throughout the town
    To whoso has not a Boeotian* ear."
I smiled appeased and with a gentle frown
    Said, "I'm the guilty poet of whom you hear."
"Good heavens," he cried, "your mantle has no nap."
    "Because my poetry's so bad," I said,
For fear again I meet with such mishap,
    Send me, I beg you, better clothes instead.

* The Boeotians were proverbially thick-witted.

318 (VI. lxxxiii)

Etruscus to his son's devotion owed
No more than, Caesar, you on both bestowed.
You hurled the flashing bolt, but soon withdrew,
'Twere good advice, if Jove should copy you.
Had he your nature, by compunction swayed
His lightnings often in mid-course had stayed.
Twice blest, Etruscus on his knees may fall;
He shared his father's exile and recall.

319 (VI. lxxxv)

Take my sixth book, Camonius, comrade dear.
Alas! 'twill never reach your kindly ear.
In luckless hour to Cappadocia stern
Sent forth, your father saw but dust return.

Reft of your own, Bononia, weep to-day;
Let mourning sound along the Aemilian way.
Alas! his piety! alas, brief span,
Scarce five Olympiads* since it first began.
You loved my trifles, knew them all by rote,
And you would reel them off without a note.
To you this booklet with my tears I send;
They are the incense of an absent friend.

* Periods of four years.

320 (VI. lxxxvi)

Full Setine bumpers strained through lordly snow,
When shall I see you and no leech say no?
Fool and ingrate, unworthy such reward,
Who'ld rather be the heir of Midas' hoard.
Spain, Asia, Libya he can have, I'm sure,
But give my enemy the hot water cure.

321 (VI. lxxxviii)

Caecilian was the name I used in lieu
Of master. 'Twas an accident, 'tis true.
What was the cost of this great liberty?
A florin less it signified to me.

322 (VI. xcii)

Myro's* serpent, Ammianus,
    Holds your chalice up:
Wine of Tuscany is in it;
    'Tis a poison cup.

* An artist in metals.

323 (VI. xciii)

Old Thais is so rank, she reeks to heaven,
Like greedy fuller's crock in pieces riven.
No hot he-goat, no lion's breath so rare
Or over-Tiber dog-skin out to air.
An ancient pickle-jar describes her best
Or unhatched chicken in forsaken nest.
To mask her odour by another stench
She doffs her robe and bathes, the dainty wench.
She's green with ointment, smeared with biting clay,
And coats of oily bean her charms array.
Let Thais play what tricks and turns she will,
The scent's breast high; she's the old vixen still.

324 (VI. xciv)

Calpetianus, still you've golden plate,
Sup you abroad or dine at home in state,
Whether afield or in a hostel small.
Has he no other? Nay, he's none at all.

325 (VII. i)

Here's the raw bull's hide of the warrior maid*,
Of which the Gorgon's angry snake's afraid.
Caesar, 'twill be a corselet when at rest;
A talisman, when gathered to your breast.

* The aegis or shield of Minerva.

326 (VII. ii)

Bane of Sarmatian arrows, stout cuirass,
Trustier than Getic war-god's shield of brass,

Against the Calydonian boar-spear* proof,
And welted deep with many a savage hoof;
Thrice happy shield upon that heart to rest,
Warmed by the pulses of that sacred breast.
Go all unscathed at his triumphant side
And give him back to peace, the victor's pride.

* The spear of Meleager, used in the fatal boar-hunt.

327 (VII. iv)

Poor Oppius, to account for his complexion,
For writing verse conceived a predilection.

328 (VII. v)

TO DOMITIAN, AT WAR IN GERMANY

Would you your people's anxious longing bless,
Caesar, our only joy and happiness,
Grant to our prayer a condescending nod;
Though triumphs come, we grudge the foe our god.
They see the World-Disposer every minute
And, though they fear his presence, revel in it.

329 (VII. vii)

The same.

Though rugged Peuce and the northern snow
And Danube with the tramp of hoofs aglow,
Or Rhine, bold, faithless, thrice in ruins hurled,
Detain the lord and master of the world,
Ruler supreme and guardian of our cares,
You cannot long be absent from our prayers.

Our eyes, our hearts, attend on Caesar still,
Alone our thoughts, our fond regrets you fill.
Let Tigris* score or Passerinus win,
The jostling circus crowd won't care a pin.

* Race-horses.

330 (VII. xii)

So may great Caesar to my playful art
Indulgent hearing, as of old, impart,
As even my foes find mercy at my hand
Nor love I any man's good name to brand.
What profits it? Some gossips many a line
Dipped in Archilochus'* poison take for mine.
Mine all this poisonous serpent's breath they say,
That cannot bear the mellowing touch of day.
You know it well, my verses have no sting,
I swear by Fame and the Castalian spring,
And by your gracious ear, to me divine,
And far from emulous hate, kind reader mine.

* The oldest Greek satirist.

331 (VII. xiii)

Hearing that Tibur would make ivory white,
    Dainty Lycoris paid a visit there.
    She left her home comparatively fair.
Alas! She soon returned as black as night.

332 (VII. xvi)

My locker's empty. For a last supply
I'll sell your presents, Regulus*. Will you buy?

* The advocate of Ep. 258.

F   8

333 (VII. xvii)

Book-room of Julius Martial's country home,
From whence the reader looks on neighbouring Rome,
If among serious poems there's a place
For the fair comic Muse's playful face,
In any pigeon-hole she'll make a shift,
With three new books, the author's loving gift.
I've read and scored them through; the writer's quill
Will give them value, though their worth were nil.
Deign to accept the dainty offering;
Your honoured name the whole wide world will sing.
A trifling pledge of friendship here they come,
Book-room of Julius Martial's country home.

334 (VII. xix)

A RELIC

This piece of useless lumber you disdain,
'Twas the first keel that sailed the uncharted main,
Which through the Clappers'* havoc landed free
And the fell anger of the Scythian sea.
Time's had his way; but though an age-worn wreck
This plank is holier than the stoutest deck.

* Fabulous rocks near the Black Sea, that caught ships between them.

335 (VII. xx)

Santra is greedy, but he's mean as well.
He rushes when he hears the dinner bell,
Reward of chase*, at eve and dewy dawn.
Four helps of loin he claims and three of brawn,

* Metaphorically, pursuit of rich men.

A hare he'll rob of wings and sirloin both,
And for a fieldfare will not spare his oath.
The blue-green beards of oysters next he grips,
And with the sweets his dirty napkin drips.
Whole jars of grapes within its folds are stored
And of pomegranate seeds a tiny hoard,
Sick figs and mushrooms and a haggis gutted,
Till, with a thousand thefts his napkin glutted,
Gnawed bones within his bosom find a bed
And a whole turtle-dove except the head.
Unblushingly his roving hand retrieves
Ungarnered scraps and what the house-dog leaves.
The solid courses are not spoil enough;
A dozen wines his borrowed flask will stuff.
He mounts two hundred steps and bars the door.
To-morrow he will sell his greedy store.

336 (VII. xxi)

All hail, thrice happy day, whose conscious birth
Gave Lucan* to his Polla and to earth.
Ah! ne'er more heinous cruel Nero's guilt;
He should have fallen ere Lucan's blood was spilt.

* The poet of the "Pharsalia," killed by Nero for conspiracy. Polla
was his widow.

337 (VII. xxii)

'Tis Lucan's day, of festivals not least;
Be present, Muses, at the joyous feast.
When to the earth that honoured name he gave
Baetis* might blend with the Castalian wave.

* The Guadalquivir, on the banks of which Lucan was born.

338 (VII. xxiii)

Phoebus, arise, as when thou didst inspire
A song of war to second Virgil's lyre*.
What is my prayer? May Polla love her lord
And may he feel that he's by her adored.

* Lucan's "Pharsalia."

339 (VII. xxv)

Your verses are insipid, mild and meek,
And whiter than the lead-beplastered cheek.
There is no tang of salt, no smack of gall,
The more fool you to wish them read at all.
No dish can spare a dash of vinegar;
No face will please without a dimple's scar.
Dull figs and honey-apples give the young;
I like my Chian to be tart and strong.

340 (VII. xxvi)

Go to Apollinaris, limping rhyme;
He won't resent it, if he has the time.
You're part his own, for better or for worse,
So to his critic eye display your verse.
If he receive you with unclouded brow
You'll ask him for his wonted favour now.
You know how he's enamoured of my line;
'Tis quite as precious in his sight as mine.
Would you disable malice for all time,
Go to Apollinaris, limping rhyme.

341 (VII. xxvii)

"A WHITE-ELEPHANT"

A Tuscan boar, full-fed with acorn feast,
A monster second to the Aetolian* beast,
Pierced by my Dexter's glittering boar-spear lies
Too great a quarry for my kitchen's prize.
Let the rich fragrance fill my steaming hall
And a whole wood to feed my kitchen fall.
What heaps of pepper the poor cook will waste!
Fish sauce, Falernian must the monster baste.
Back to your lord. My shallow fire-side spare,
Unthrifty boar! Starvation's cheaper fare.

* The Calydonian boar. Ep. 326.

342 (VII. xxviii)

So may your Tibur forest thrive for you
And your cut coppice its staddles quick renew,
Your olive, Fuscus, vie with Spain divine
And teeming vats brim high with luscious wine,
So may the palace praise, the crowd adore,
And many a garland wreath your threshold o'er;
While merry Christmas* lends you time to waste,
Review my quips with your unfailing taste.
"Truth's a hard matter." That's as it may be,
You like to hear it; speak it then to me.

* See Ep. 213.

343 (VII. xxxi)

New-laid eggs and cackling chicken,
Yellow figs just ripe to pick in,
Tender kid of bleating goat,
Olive in his winter coat,

Greens with Christmas hoar-frost yellow,
Home-bred? Not a bit, dear fellow.
Regulus, you court disaster,
My farm bears nothing but its master.
All that to your door may come
From Umbria, Cales, Tusculum,
Etruria or the third milestone,
Suburra yields to me alone.

344 (VII. xxxii)

A MODEL YOUNGSTER

Atticus, scion of an ancient tree,
Not brooking your great house should silent be,
Minerva's grateful satellites attend you,
Philosophy and studious ease befriend you.
While other youths to battered trainers fly
And greasy oilers drain their treasury dry,
At tennis or at football you'll not toil
Or woo the bath with stroke of blunted foil;
Your arms in supple boxing you'll not square,
Nor pass the dusty hand-ball everywhere,
But hurry to the Maiden's Pool* of snow
Or where Europa's bull† with love's aglow.
Who squanders leisure on such vulgar sport,
When he may run, forgets that life is short.

* The reservoir of the aqueduct of Agrippa, called thus for its purity.
† A lounge near the Pincian Hill.

345 (VII. xxxiii)

Seeing your coat's so filthy, as you know,
Your shoe more white than freshly fallen snow,
Why trail your dirty robe? I caution you,
Kilt up your gown or you will spoil your shoe.

346 (VII. xxxvi)

ONE GOOD TURN DESERVES ANOTHER

Unable to endure the constant strain,
When my rough villa swam with winter rain,
Against the sudden storms to make a shift
A shower of tiles came to me as a gift.
December's blast roars loud and fast and faster;
Stella, you thatch the house but not the master.

347 (VII. xxxvii)

You know, my friend, the quaestor's fatal sign;
Here's a new hint for punishment condign.
Each time his nose, bedewed with cold, he blew
'Twas a death-warrant by a precedent new.
An icicle congealed by winter snows
Hung—an unsightly pendant—from his nose.
His colleagues held his hands. The end? You know it.
His nose, poor fellow, why, he couldn't blow it.

348 (VII. xxxviii)

Severus, Polyphemus really might,
He's such a freak, the Cyclops' self affright.
And Scylla's such another. Join the pair
And each will give the other fits, I swear.

349 (VII. xxxix)

Weary of wandering through the dregs of night,
Of patron's notice and of rich man's slight,
Coelius feigns the gout, but to make sure
Besmears and binds with lint and ligature,

Halting and hobbling with laborious tread
As if he really ought to be in bed.
See the stern doom for trickery decreed;
For his sham gout he now has gout indeed.

350 (VII. xl)

Here lies Etruscus, known to Caesar's court,
Who proudly bore frail fortune's fickle sport.
His duteous sons have laid them side by side,
Husband and wife; their souls in heaven abide.
She perished first, cut off in early prime.
Full seventy years were his allotted time.
Who saw your tears, Etruscus*, he in truth
Would think your sire cut off in budding youth.

* The son.

351 (VII. xli)

A play on the word *cosmos* meaning "world" or "toilet" (cosmetics).

The world's your perfume-jar; no comment add,
Tucca; the world holds perfumes good and bad.

352 (VII. xlii)

If anyone in gifts would vie with you
He'ld dare you, Castricus, in poems too.
We're humble folk; we cannot give or write;
Hence our deep sleep and calm repose at night.
"Why send you my poor verses?" you would say.
Fruit to Alcinous*? Yet perhaps one may.

* Coals to Newcastle.

353 (VII. xliv)

A PORTRAIT

Ovid, your own Caesonius here you see,
    Whose features in the breathing wax are shown.
Nero condemned him, but you dared to be
    Loyal and share an exile not your own;
Through Scylla's gulf* you followed on his way,
    Though you refused to hear his Consul's call.
If any part of me is doomed to stay,
    And these my verses to survive at all,
Then shall the tale be told nor ever end,
That he was Seneca's, you his trusty friend.

* The Straits of Messina, on his way to banishment in Africa.

354 (VII. xlv)

Of eloquent Seneca the noble friend,
More than Secundus dear, to whom he penned
Full many a kindly page in letters white,
Caesonius Maximus* here greets our sight.
Through Sicily's strait you still were faithful found,
Ovid, a name for all the world to sound.
You spurned the madman's wrath. Let Hellas praise
Pylades, loyal friend of other days.
'Twas Clytemnestra's exiled son he tended;
You savage Nero's victim still befriended.

* The friend of Ovid above mentioned.

355 (VII. xlvi)

You'll send your present with a verse to me;
Fain would you rival Homer's poetry.

At my expense your Muse is silent still;
Day in, day out, you torture me at will.
To wealthy friends send verse and elegies;
A beggar needs more solid gifts than these.

356 (VII. xlvii)

Sura, supreme in learning justly held,
Whose speech recalls the sober days of eld,
How kind a fate did your sad ghost redeem
Snatched from the brink of the Lethean stream.
Our tears had lost their sting; we felt no dread
In our distress: you were already dead.
Avernus' ruler, fearful of our scorn,
Gave back the thread the fates had well-nigh shorn.
You know your death moved all men's hearts to sorrow,
And you enjoy the homage of to-morrow.
Live on your spoil, be happy while you may;
Life given back can't waste a single day.

357 (VII. xlviii)

Annius has many tables, pages try
Their best to serve them, plates and dishes fly.
To acrobatic feasts let the rich man turn;
I hate a meal that's like a Jack-o'-lantern.

358 (VII. xlix)

Would these suburban gifts Severus charm,
The eggs will do him good, the fruit no harm.

359 (VII. li)

To buy my rubbish you perhaps may shun,
Though willing, Urbicus, to share the fun.
To Auctus haste—I think you know the way—
Within the Avenger's* gate he sits all day;
Learned in law and eloquent to plead,
He's not my reader but my book indeed.
He knows my rhymes and quotes them all by heart;
Of all my lines there fails no single part.
To claim their authorship he's no delight
Or steal my reputation, though he might.
Go seek him out and share his frugal store,
But not too early; he'll be free at four.
You drink, he'll spout and spout, though you rebuff,
And spout and spout, when you cry "Hold, enough!"

* The temple of Mars Ultor in commemoration of Philippi.

360 (VII. lii)

You read my books to Celer. Well and good,
If Celer likes them, be it understood.
My own Iberians his justice know;
Such spotless faith not all the world can show.
I dread his kindly censure all the more:
He'll be a critic, not an auditor.

361 (VII. liii)

Umber, at Christmas time you sent my way
The garnered harvest of the holiday*.
Seven toothpicks, tablets twelve a parcel made
With napkins, goblet, and a sponge to aid.

* For clients' presents, compare Ep. 186: these were sent on to Martial.

Beans, olives in Picenian wicker-ware
And jars of Spain's dark desiccate were there.
Home figs and gathered on the Egyptian shore
With yellow damsons swelled the rustic store.
A crown, methinks, would buy the precious freight
Borne on the backs of hulking Syrians eight.
What waste of toil! Best send, your pains to spare
Five pounds of silver that a slave can bear.

362 (VII. liv)

Each morn your dreams of me you still recite
To make each several hair stand up with fright.
Last vintage and this year's have long gone dry,
For some old witch to charm the omen by.
I've squandered salt-cakes, incense heaps, and all
My flocks are spent, so fast the younglings fall.
No pig is left, no egg, chick old or young.
Nasidienus, wake or hold your tongue.

363 (VII. lvi)

Rabirius*, faithful student of the sky,
Building a palace with skilled artistry,
If Pisa† would erect a worthy shrine
For Jove of Phidias, the task were thine.

* Who built a dome for Domitian.
† Famous for Phidias' bust of Zeus Olympios.

364 (VII. lx)

Lord of the Capitol*, if our belief
Hold you omnipotent, protect our chief.
Each pours his earnest pleadings in your ear
With such entreaties as a god can hear.

* Jupiter.

If for myself no humble plea I make,
Forgive me nor my modesty mistake.
For Caesar I am bound to pray to you,
But for myself my prayer's to Caesar due.

365 (VII. lxi)

THE STREETS CLEARED OF HAWKERS

When fussy hawkers had beset the town
And none could call his dwelling-place his own,
Caesar, new highways you on us bestowed
And what was once a lane became a road.
No tavern-pest is girt with pots in rows,
No jostled Praetor down the kennel goes.
Knife-grinders in the turmoil ply no trade,
No filthy cookshop clogs the esplanade.
Each barber, vintner, butcher, dwells at home;
'Twas a vast shop, 'tis now imperial Rome.

366 (VII. lxiii)

If thou may'st Silius' deathless epic* read,
Fit monument of Latium's ancient breed,
Think not he covets Bacchus' wreaths alone,
And claims the Muses' refuge as his own;
He did not venture Virgil's stately art
Till he had mighty Cicero by heart.
The learned council love to twine his bays
And many a grateful client sings his praise.
Consul he was in that world-famous year†
Which gave us liberty and calmed our fear.
Life's lees he gave to Phoebus and the Muses,
And for the law-court Helicon he chooses.

* The "Punic Wars." Silius was an advocate.
† The year of Nero's death.

367 (VII. lxiv)

> A barber once, our city's chief delight,
> Now by your mistress' bounty made a knight,
> Spurning the forum and the law's delay
> To Sicily, Cinnamus*, you took your way.
> How shall you kill long years in idleness,
> How has your truant leisure power to bless?
> Stoic or Cynic is beyond your reach,
> You cannot plead, you cannot train or teach
> Or for provincial actors clap and bawl.
> One place is left for you, the barber's stall!
> * Ep. 284.

368 (VII. lxv)

> Gargilianus, well you may lament
> Those twenty years that on one suit you spent;
> Still it's your fault; defeat is not a crime,
> And for such victories one has not time.

369 (VII. lxvi)

A FORTUNE-HUNTER'S LAMENT

> Fabius left Labienus all his store;
> He says that no investment cost him more.

370 (VII. lxix)

> Your bride Theophila is here;
> Athenian born she might appear.
> Plato would claim her of his crew,
> The Stoics bid her welcome too.
> So shrewd her sense, her taste so high,
> To her addressed no work will die;

Pantaenis, though the Muses love her,
Canius, could never rank above her.
If Phaon* Sappho's verse allure,
She's not less learned and more pure.

* Sappho's swain.

371 (VII. lxxii)

Well, Paulus, here's a happy Christmas Day*;
May no cheap clouts or tablets come your way†,
No poor half-pounds of pepper be your fate,
But piles of dishes and ancestral plate
From some rich culprit or more potent friend,
Or some delicious cate your fare to mend.
May Novius and Publius confess
You are their conqueror at draughts and chess;
From the unwashed to you the verdict fall
For active service with the playful ball;
May you not yield to Polybus' left-hand swing;
Premised that, if one says my verses sting,
You back me up, and shout with all your might,
"Such scurril stuff my Martial did not write."

* Ep. 213.
† For presents to lawyers, compare Ep. 186. There were of course no fees.

372 (VII. lxxiii)

The Esquiline and Aventine are yours
And the Patrician Street* confronts your doors;
Thence widowed Cybele and Vesta's fire
And ancient Jove and modern you admire.
Where shall I meet you, whither, pray, repair?
He has no home who lodges everywhere.

* Under the Esquiline hill.

373 (VII. lxxviii)

TOO KIND BY HALF

A lizard's tail from Sex* with you is seen
And for a bean-feast oil besmeared on bean.
Each dainty dish becomes your neighbour's prize:
You're neither merry, Papilus, nor wise.

* In Southern Spain (Paley).

374 (VII. lxxix)

Consular wine, nectar divine,
That is the stuff that you drink when you dine.
Wine to revere—what do I hear?
Consul and namesake are both of this year.

375 (VII. lxxx)

Since Roman peace reigns by the northern star*
And hushed is all the trumpet-blare of war,
Pray, good Faustinus, send my little rhyme
To Marcellinus, now he'll have the time.
But, if my humble present you'ld commend,
For kindness sake a youthful carrier send,
Not one who, fed on milk of Scythian mare,
Skims o'er the ice upon his rolling chair,
But ruddy stripling or of Lesbian strain,
Or Spartan, yet untaught to suffer pain†.
He'll send some captive boy from Danube's tide‡
To tend his master's flocks on Tibur's side.

* Peace with the Dacians.
† Alluding to the scourging inflicted on all Spartan boys.
‡ A Dacian prisoner.

376 (VII. lxxxiii)

Prettywit the barber
   Dabbed Lupercus' face.
When he got round, new hair he found
   Growing in the old hair's place*.

* It was such a long way round.

377 (VII. lxxxiv)

My portrait, painted for Secundus dear,
A living, breathing masterpiece is here.
Meanwhile, my book, to Peuce*, Danube wend;
Those vanquished realms are governed by my friend.
Gift small but welcome to my comrade go,
And in thy verse a livelier image show.
Proof against chance, against destroying time,
Beyond Apelles'† span will live my rhyme.

* An island in the Danube.
† Who painted Alexander of Macedon.

378 (VII. lxxxvi)

Once, Sextus, when we knew each other least,
You would invite me to your birthday feast.
After long years, what moment mischief-fraught
Made ancient fellowship to count for nought?
I know the reason, 'tis because I send
No Spanish frosted gold to please my friend;
No tidy coat or mantle comes your way.
That is no gift, for which one has to pay.
That plan will bring you presents, friends 'twill not.
Go whip your slave, and say "The rogue forgot."

379 (VII. lxxxvii)

If Flaccus mine a long-eared goat-fox loves,
If Canius' breast a cross-grained Kafir moves,
If Publius admires a pigmy pup,
If Cronius with his brother ape takes up,
If Marius for the foul ichneumon dies,
If Lausus loves the voice of chattering pies,
If round Glaucilla's neck cold serpents trail
And Telesina mourns a nightingale,
Why not admire Labyca's winsome face,
When such abortions find with others grace?

380 (VII. lxxxviii)

My verse is found to be, or rumour lies,
Of fair Vienna* the delight and prize.
By son and sire and grandsire I'm adored,
Conned by the chaste wife with her crusty lord.
'Tis better thus than if my books were read
By those who drink at Nilus' fountain-head,
Than if my Tagus drenched me with his ore,
Hybla, Hymettus gave my bees their store.
I'm something then, my faith is not amiss,
I must believe you, Lausus, after this†.

* On the Rhone.
† Lausus had said the book contained 30 bad epigrams, implying that
    that was all.

381 (VII. lxxxix)

Go, happy rose, with many a pliant spray
    Enwreath my friend Apollinaris' hair,
Still bind it long years hence when it is grey:
    So be you ever dear to Venus fair.

382 (VII. xc)

I write unequal verse, so Matho says;
If it be true his criticism's a praise.
Try Umber, Cluvienus by that test:
No, Creticus; bad's bad; good seldom best.

383 (VII. xcii)

"If you're in want, you know you needn't ask,"
    So, Baccara, you say twice, thrice a day.
My banker takes me churlishly to task;
    You hear, but don't know what I want, you say.
My landlord duns me when you're standing by;
    You hear him, Baccara, and say "What's this?"
"My mantle's cold and threadbare too," I cry;
    You hear, and still you wonder what's amiss.
You wonder. Would some planet might be got
To strike you dumb, you and your "wonder what."

384 (VII. xciii)

Narnia, engirt with sulphur waters bright,
Scarce to be scaled from height to perilous height,
What ails thee, Quintus* thus to steal away
And his returning footsteps still delay?
Why rob my little farm of all its pleasure?
My neighbour then was all my joy and treasure.
Forbear and trespass not upon your guest;
So may your bridge† on piers of adamant rest.

---

* Quintus Ovidius of Epp. 472 and 541.
† Across the river Nar and continued by viaducts among the hills.

385 (VII. xcvi)

Here lie I, Urbicus, true son of Rome*,
Young Urbicus, new grief of Bassus' home.
Six months were lacking to my first three years,
The cruel sisters plied their ruthless shears.
What did my beauty, wit and age avail?
Weep at my tomb all ye who read the tale.
So may all those you'ld have in life to stay
Beyond old Nestor's span grim Death delay.

* The meaning of Urbicus, "one of the city."

386 (VII. xcvii)

You know Sabinus well, my rhyme,
Glory of Umbria's mountain clime,
Townsman of Pudens, friend of old.
To seek him, though engaged, be bold.
Though cares and troubles throng about him,
He'll read my verses, never doubt him.
He loves me dearly, holds me next
In rank to Turnus'* noble text.
What readers shall I find, what fame!
Banquet and court will sound my name.
House, porch and shop and lounge will heed you,
You're sent to one, the world will read you.

* An unknown satirist.

387 (VII. xcviii)

Castor buys all he sees. 'Tis plain
What Castor buys he'll sell again.

388 (VII. xcix)

Crispinus*, so may you the Thunderer kind
And Rome as friendly as your Memphis find,
If in the palace halls my verse you hear,
For 'tis familiar to that sacred ear,
Be bold to say, a critic kind as fair,
"This poet's worth your reading anywhere.
With Marsus he or learn'd Catullus vies."
No more. In higher hands the sequel lies.

* An Egyptian of low extraction now in great power.

389 (VIII. iii)

ADDRESSED TO HIS VOLUMES OF VERSE

Once you were five; you ran to six and seven;
Too much. You'll still be spouting, gracious heaven!
For shame, an end! I've glory and to spare.
Enough! I'm read and cherished everywhere
When old Messala's pillars melt away,
When Licinus' marble crumbles to decay,
I'll still be sung. The sojourner at Rome
Will bear me with him to his distant home.
Thus I. The eldest of the Nine replied,
Her perfumed locks and robe with spikenard dyed,
"Thankless, will you forsake your pleasant rhyme?
How better should you spend your leisure time?
What? Change your motley for the tragic train
And sing of savage wars in Epic strain,
For some hoarse, puffing pedant to dictate
And every full-grown lad and lass to hate?
In themes like those let the o'er-strict delight,
Poor things, who burn the wakeful oil by night.

Your verses should be spiced with Roman wit,
And let your book our social fashions fit.
What though to humble pitch its note be set?
Your reed will silence many a clarion yet."

390 (VIII. vi)

All your antiques, Euctus, I cannot bear;
Give me a Toby jug of earthenware.
You flaunt the musty pedigree of your plate;
The very wine grows sick to hear you prate.
"To coax it from Laomedon, my boy,
Apollo's harp upreared the walls of Troy.
See, with this bowl stout Rhoecus* fought that day
The Lapithae: 'tis battered by the fray.
Those double cups from veteran Priam come;
Doves—*ecce signum*—fretted by his thumb.
And in this goblet, his good friends to please,
A noble wassail poured Aeacides†.
Fair Dido too, when great Aeneas' host,
Pledged Bitias here in a full brimming toast."
Your wine such ancient testimony lacks;
From Priam's cup you drink Astyanax‡.

* A centaur.   † Achilles.
‡ Hector's infant son.

391 (VIII. vii)

Cinna, is this your eloquence, I pray,
To stammer out some half-score words a day?
That shout betrayed you. Four court days you ask.
Four days of silence? Cinna, what a task!

392 (VIII. viii)

JANUARY: DOMITIAN RETURNING FROM THE GERMAN
CAMPAIGN

Though, Janus, you renew the flying years,
    Though from your godhead passing winters date,
Incense salute you first, prayers greet your ears,
    Consuls pay homage and each magistrate,
You're gladder for Rome's happiness to learn
That in your moon we see our lord's return.

393 (VIII. x)

Fine Tyrian mantles Bassus lately bought;
    Ten thousand sesterces the price, men say.
He made a bargain. "It was cheap, you thought?"
    Cheap? Oh dear no! Only the man won't pay.

394 (VIII. xii)

Why not marry money? 'Tis more in my way
To love and to cherish than love and obey.
For a match to be equal, in person and purse
A man's better half should be rather the worse.

395 (VIII. xiii)

I bought a fool for twenty thousand cool;
Pay back, Gargilianus. He's no fool.

396 (VIII. xiv)

Lest with the cold your Eastern fruit decay
    Or your young woodland wilt in winter's bite,
A green-house mantling o'er each tender spray
    Basks in the south and lets in purest light.

A garret's mine half open to the sky,
  Wherein the North Wind would not bide a week.
Fie on such cruelty to an old ally!
  With your own trees a tighter roof I'll seek.

397 (VIII. xv)

For our Pannonian victories we pour
Offering to Jove, who saved our emperor.
Knights offer incense, people, senate too,
The humblest Roman shares the gracious dew.
But laurelled peace has victories as well
And with unspoken joy our bosoms swell
That in your flock such confidence is shown.
The royal shepherd he, who knows his own.

398 (VIII. xvi)

Cyperus, baker once, pleader to-day,
    Earning a fortune and as quickly squandering,
    And borrowing, from the baker never wandering,
  Still you make bread and still you clear the tray

399 (VIII. xvii)

Two thousand* was the fee for your defence:
    You sent but one; the reason, Sextus, pray?
"You never spoke, you gave my case away."
    You owe me double for my reticence.
  * £16.

400 (VIII. xviii)

Cyrenius, you might publish and attain
A vogue like mine or higher, but refrain.
So dear you prize my honour, that my fame
You more esteem than your own honoured name.

So Virgil would not write in Horace' style
Though he might vie with Pindar's self the while,
And hushed a note of more majestic tone
That Varius might possess the stage alone.
Gold, wealth, estates will many a man resign
To save a friend, but few the bay divine.

401 (VIII. xx)

Varus, two hundred lines each day that flies
You write and burn. How foolish—and how wise!

402 (VIII. xxi)

ON DOMITIAN RETURNING FROM DACIA

Daystar, give back the daylight. Why delay?
Caesar draws nigh. Daystar, give back the day.
Rome needs you. Does the lazy Northern star
With lagging steeds detain your lingering car?
The heavenly Castor, of your need aware,
From Leda's stable Cyllarus* might spare.
Why stay the eager sun? Night's armies flit,
Xanthus and Aethon† champ the foaming bit,
Yet daylight lingers and no star gives place,
The moon would see our sovereign face to face.
Great Caesar, dawn upon your people's sight;
Though heaven be darkened, they will find it light.

* Castor, Leda his mother, and Cyllarus his horse were all turned into
  stars.
† The horses of the sun.

403 (VIII. xxii)

You serve a squeaker for a royal boar.
If I'm deceived, a Jew's my ancestor

404 (VIII. xxiii)

A brute am I, to bring the rogue to book
Who spoiled the supper, and too fond of eating?
If food's a trifle, how can any cook
Deserve a beating?

405 (VIII. xxiv)

TO DOMITIAN

If my poor slender volume pleads for me,
Pray do not think it importunity.
The plea admit, though you the gift refuse;
Great Jove no incense and no prayer eschews.
A god's not made by gold and sculptor's art;
He makes a god, who asks what's in his heart.

406 (VIII. xxvi)

Full oft in terror by the Ganges bed
The tiger-hunter from his prey has fled,
But Rome could witness at Domitian's feast
Wonders more countless than the savage East.
Your Circus, Caesar, passes Bacchus' show,
His pomp and affluence of long ago.
When he dragged India captive from his war,
One pair of tigers drew his gorgeous car.

407 (VIII. xxviii)

For Parthenius, see Ep. 217.

New toga, present from an eloquent friend,
To what famed flock fresh lustre wilt thou lend?
Did Greek Tarentum weave thy texture rare,
Whose fields are watered by Galaesus fair?

Or Baetis*, guardian of the western plain,
Infuse thy living fleece with snowy grain?
Did many-mouthed Timavus know thee first,
Where starry, faithful Cyllarus† quenched his thirst?
Thou wast too precious for the Spartan dye;
No Tyrian purple flaws thy chastity.
Thou art as lily or fresh privet white
Or ivory sheen of Tibur's marble height;
Whiter than Paphos' doves or Spartan swan
Or pearls from Indian ocean ever shone.
Well may its snowy brightness bring to mind,
Parthenius, thy spirit just and kind.
Not Babylon's woof is half so fair, I wis,
Wrought by the needle of Semiramis.
In Phrixus' golden fleece‡ were I arrayed,
This robe would put such raiment in the shade.
A merry spectacle, I ween, to see
This mantle with that robe in company.

* A Spanish river famous for its flocks.
† Castor's horse. Ep. 402.
‡ The fleece brought by Jason from Colchis.

408 (VIII. XXX)

A MODERN SCAEVOLA IN THE ROMAN AMPHITHEATRE

What Brutus' days accounted high renown
Is now the sport and pleasure of the town.
See how one hand basks in the fiery shame
Stoutly and triumphs o'er the astonished flame.
See how the victim gazes when it burns
And the red sacrifice to pleasure turns.
More stubborn yet, did not some power restrain,
His left upon the wearied hearth had lain.

Let former deeds, brave hand, remain untold;
Enough the marvel that these eyes behold.

409 (VIII. xxxii)

A gentle dove down through the silent sky
We saw to Aratulla's bosom fly.
'Twas no mere chance, for unobserved it stayed
A willing prisoner of the pensive maid.
If fate may heed a loyal sister's care,
If the world's sovereign may be moved by prayer,
The feathered harbinger from Sardis flew
Cooing "Your brother* will return to you."

* Now in exile.

410 (VIII. xxxiii)

A sample from the praetor's crown*, my friend,
'Tis to pass current for a bowl, you send.
With such a film the stage-machine† was plated,
By pale red saffron rain-drops dissipated.
Say, was it scraped by cunning page-boy's nail,
This airy cutting, from your sofa-rail?
'Twill feel the blast of a mosquito's wing;
A butterfly will set it quivering;
It flutters in a tiny lantern's breath;
Spill but one drop of wine, 'tis doomed to death.
Clad in such film the date on New Year's Day
With thrifty pence the unkempt clients pay.
Less thin the thread that Egypt's bean‡ supplies,
Less frail the lily that with sunshine dies.

* Of threaded gold leaf.
† A crane used in pageants.
‡ It could be drawn out like gut.

Thicker on old Fabulla's face the cake,
Less frail the bubble when you stir a lake.
Stronger the bladder ordered tresses wear,
And the Dutch soap that dyes our ladies' hair.
In such a skin is swathed a chick unhatched,
With such a crescent are our foreheads patched.
But why a bowl when you a spoon might send—
An egg-spoon if you will—my lavish friend?
I soar too high: Paulus, a snail-shell small
You might have sent, or nothing, friend, at all.

411 (VIII. xxxiv)

Of ancient plate you call yourself a hoarder.
Precisely, if it were not made to order.

412 (VIII. xxxv)

Bad wife, bad husband, like as pea to pea,
I really wonder that you can't agree.

413 (VIII. xxxvi)

DOMITIAN'S NEW PALACE

Caesar, at wondrous pyramids you smile
And eastern monuments of dusky Nile;
Egyptian handiwork is here outdone,
And all that's fairest underneath the sun.
You'ld think Rome's hills united in its floor
More high than Ossa when it Pelion bore.
So tall it towers that, shrouded mid the stars,
The roof serene looks down on lightning's wars.

Earlier 'tis bathed in Phoebus' new-born ray
Than Circe can behold the rising day.
This palace, lifting star-encircled brows
As high as heaven, to its great author bows.

414 (VIII. xxxvii)

To Caietanus you give back his bill
    And think a hundred thousand you restore.
"A debt," you say. Keep, Polycharmus, still
    Your bond and lend the man two thousand more.

415 (VIII. xxxviii)

He, who with ceaseless benefits should load
One not insensible of service owed,
Perchance might favour or requital claim,
But he, who after death endows a name,
What profit seeks he but to assuage his woe?
Being good is better far than seeming so.
Melior, we know full well the dead you cherish
And will not suffer Plancus' name to perish;
Dispensing gifts upon his natal day
To grateful fellow-scribes, "His feast," you say.
This, while your life is spared, will bring you fame
And after death win honour for your name.

416 (VIII. xxxix)

Till now there was no corner anywhere
For the imperial feast's ambrosial fare.
Here, Caesar, you the nectar cup may sip,
With Ganymede himself to crown its lip.
Long may it be or ere you dine above.
You're in a hurry? Come and fetch him, Jove.

417 (VIII. xl)

Priapus*, keeper of no garden fair
Or wealthy vineyard, but of woodland rare
Whence you came forth, from whence may be renewed,
Fend off, I warn you, pilfering fingers rude,
And keep my spinney for its lord's employ.
If firewood fails, well, you're a log, my boy.

* A god whose wooden statue guarded boundaries. Compare Ep. 601.

418 (VIII. xli)

At Christmas* time no present did I get
From Athenagoras, "much to his regret."
Whether he's really sorry I don't know.
One thing is certain, he has made me so.

* Ep. 213.

419 (VIII. xlii)

A BID FOR A CLIENT

Matho, unless some richer bait allure you,
A hundred baths* my bounty shall secure you.

* At a farthing.

420 (VIII. xliii)

Chrestilla lays her lords to rest, his ladies
Fabius, and ushers them with pomp to Hades.
Kind Venus, match the winners. Then, I trust,
One funeral pyre will turn the pair to dust.

421 (VIII. xliv)

Titullus, live; to live is all too late.
Begin at school, it is a lagging date.

Wretch, you don't live, although your hair be grey,
But pay your early greeting every day.
Each morning you, with slobbering kisses wet,
Around the courts and mounted statues sweat,
Caesar's Colossus and the war-god's home;
From thence till noon you scour the streets of Rome.
Seize, heap, secure, possess; you'll leave your store.
What though your chest's abrim with yellow ore,
Though to your shade a hundred debts are due,
Your heir will warrant you not worth a sou.
When you are lying on the marble cold,
Or bed of state displays your lifeless mould,
When, paper-lined, the funeral pile shall rise,
With rude salute he'll mock the mourners' sighs.

422 (VIII. xlv)

Priscus is back from Sicily to his own.
I'll mark the day with many a milk-white stone.
Through linen strained the trickling cask shall flow,
Shrunk by a hundred consulships or so.
When will my tables with such radiance shine,
Or lips more fitly glow with ruddy wine?
Flaccus, when Cyprus gives you back to me,
You'll be such cause for mirth and jollity.

423 (VIII. xlviii)

Crispinus knows not who has got his cloak,
    Changing his dress to don his gown* for dinner.
Somebody, give it back! 'Tis past a joke.
    The cloak and not the owner tracks the sinner.

* Or toga.

The garment's delicate with purple grain,
   A hue more suitable to high condition.
If you're so much in love with sordid gain,
   Resume the toga, to avoid suspicion.

424 (VIII. li)

Saucer, you were of Mys' or Myro's hand,
By Mentor or by Polycletus planned.
Fresh and untarnished you will think no shame
To swelter in the assayer's scorching flame.
Less fair the pure electron's yellow glow,
And ivory dims beside your silver snow.
The workmanship's as rare. The sheen less bright
When round us gleams the full-orbed moon at night.
Fit ferryman for Helle* stands a goat
Mantled in Theban Phrixus'† golden coat.
Cinyphian herd‡ such heavenly fleece would spare,
Nor Bacchus§ grudge his vineyard's use to share.
Upon his back Love rides with golden wings,
Between whose lips Apollo's reed-pipe rings:
So glad the dolphin through the Lesbian deep
Bare sweet Arion‖ over waves asleep.
Fill high the princely gift with nectar rare,
No common slave-boy but my Cestus fair.
Cestus, a Setine bumper, let it float!
The boy's athirst, so is the golden goat.
A measure for each letter let me lift
Of Rufus Instans for his royal gift.

* As white as the ram that was to bear Helle across the Hellespont.
† Helle's brother, who left the fleece in Colchis.
‡ Cilician goat-herd.
§ Goats preyed on young vine-shoots.
‖ The bard of Lesbos, saved from drowning by a dolphin.

If Telethusa's coming glad my door,
I'll dip four times* to Rufus, only four.
In doubt, 'twill stretch to seven. Is she unkind?
Four times and seven shall bring me peace of mind.

* *I.e.* Mix water with four parts wine out of twelve.

425 (VIII. lii)

A barber lad, who worthily had sheared
The cheek of Nero and the Claudian beard,
Caedicianus, I to Rufus lent,
Of such rare skill to make experiment.
While he removed the outgrowth strand by strand
Steered by the mirror in the critic's hand,
Rouging his cheeks and slaying thrice the slain,
A man full-bearded he came home again.

426 (VIII. lv)

Loud as the crash on pathless Libya's shore,
What time the wood hears myriad lions roar,
And the pale neatherd to their wonted stalls
His frightened steers and wildered heifers calls,
So loud a thunder through our circus stirred;
It was but one, you'ld take it for a herd.
One, but whole troops would own his mandate dread
And marbled Afric's diadem grace his head.
That royal mane, shading his shaggy breast,
And crescent glory of his golden chest!
How well his bulk became the hunting spear!
How he faced death in triumph, not in fear!
Whence, Libya, came this glory from afar
To your wild woods? Came it from Cybele's car*?
Or, Caesar, did your brother† from on High
Or father send this monster from the sky?

* Drawn by lions.   † Hercules. See note on Ep. 479.

427 (VIII. lvi)

To our own age our ancestors give way
And Rome is waxing with her lord to-day.
You marvel that the gift of Maro* passed
And no man reawakes his trumpet blast.
Give us Maecenas, Flaccus, Maro'll come;
You'll rear a Virgil in your country home.
Poor Tityrus† had lost his farm and stock
Hard by Cremona and bewailed his flock:
The kind knight‡ smiles and bids grim poverty
Pack off and want on timorous pinion flee.
"Be rich," he said, "of poets unsurpassed,
And keep your love for our Alexis§ fast."
He at his master's board was wont to stand
And pour dark nectar with a lily hand.
Even Jove himself might not disdain to sip
The cup that once had touched his dainty lip.
Amazed, the poet nut-brown Thestylis
Can spare, nor fat-cheeked Galatea miss.
The buzzing gnat's no more his tearful theme;
Italy, arms, the man are all his dream‖.
Why tell of Varius, Marsus, honoured roll?
It were great labour to recount the scroll.
If you're Maecenas, shall I Virgil be?
Virgil? Oh, no! But Marsus certainly.

* Virgil.
† The shepherd in Virgil's eclogues, representing himself.
‡ Virgil's patron Maecenas.
§ A favourite boy of Tityrus.
‖ Subjects of the *Aeneid*.

428 (VIII. lvii)

> Old Picens had three teeth and spat them out
>   While seated on the margin of his grave;
> Soon marked and gathered as they lay about
>   And to the relics decent burial gave.
> His future heir these bones need not collect;
> Picens has paid himself this last respect.

429 (VIII. lviii)

> So thick, Artemidorus, is your cloak
> That I might call you coarsehair* for a joke.

* Play on a Scythian word for "cloak."

430 (VIII. lix)

> You see that ugly Cyclops, on whose face
> A bleary gulf gapes in one optic's place?
> Despise him not, he's sharp beyond belief;
> Autolycus was not so rare a thief.
> Well, watch him closely, when he dines with you;
> He's on the job—one eye's as good as two.
> Your anxious slaves miss many a spoon and cup,
> In his warm cloak·napkins are smothered up.
> His neighbour slips a mantle; 'tis his prey,
> And often doubly swathed he goes away.
> A boy takes forty winks; his torch he'll steal;
> The thing may be ablaze; he'll do the deal.
> All failing, he'll some crafty moment choose,
> Outwit the slave and snatch the owner's shoes.

431 (VIII. lxi)

Charinus frets and fumes and weeps at me
And fain would dangle on some lofty tree;
Not that I'm read and sung the wide world through,
Well oiled with cedar and with bosses new,
And scattered broadcast; but to think that I've
A house near town and my own mule-team drive.
Envy, Severus, should receive its due:
Grant him, ye gods, a team and villa too.

432 (VIII. lxii)

On verses' backs to write is Picens' whim;
His art, offended, turns its back on him.

433 (VIII. lxiv)

Each year, to bounty to incite us,
You have eight birthday feasts, my Clytus;
Not only two or three or four
But, Clytus, many birthdays more.
What though your face be smoother far
Than pearls from the arid ocean are,
Black as ripe mulberry each tress,
Like softest down your daintiness,
Or cone of curdled cheese, your chest
Swelling like full-grown maiden's breast?
Yet you seem old to us. In age
You're Priam's self or Nestor sage.
A truce to all this theft, I pray;
But if you will play out the play
And think one birth a year's too small,
I'll think you have no birth* at all.

* No honourable birth. Compare Ep. 103.

434 (VIII. lxvi)

Incense and offerings to Augustus* bring,
Ye Muses, for your Silius' honouring.
His son is consul and the poet's home
Now bears again the noble rods of Rome.
Caesar, our only stay, he's yet one prayer,
That his young son the consulship may share.
The sires to Pompey gave a three-fold lease,
Caesar † to Agrippa in the year of peace.
Silius, himself once consul, fain would see
His mantle resting on his family.

* Domitian: in his case Augustus is the imperial title.
† Augustus founder of the empire.

435 (VIII. lxvii)

Ere yet an hour to noon you tap the door
A most unwelcome early visitor;
Before the pleader voids the court and when
The Floral circus matches beasts and men*.
Callistus, quick! rout out my unwashed crew.
Prepare the couches. Pray be seated, do.
"Warm water!" There's no water anywhere;
The kitchen's empty, and the hearth is bare.
Come earlier still; why linger till eleven?
Come rather with the breakfast things at seven.

* The games at the festival of Flora.

436 (VIII. lxviii)

Who should behold Alcinous' garden fair
Would think yours nobler far beyond compare.
Lest chilling frost its ripening clusters blight
Or Bacchus' bounty feel the winter's spite,

Transparent crystal guards the purple rows
And still unhid the prosperous vintage grows.
So through her silk a woman's charms appear
And pebbles shimmer in the streamlet clear.
Complaisant Nature still to genius bows,
And barren Yule with autumn's wealth endows.

437 (VIII. lxx)

Our gentle Nerva has both force and wit,
But to his eloquence applies the bit.
He might drink deeply of Castalia's well,
But takes a simpler draught his thirst to quell,
Content to wreath his brow with modest bay
Nor the full canvas of his fame display.
Yet may his name as our Tibullus go
With those who Nero's* flowery pages know.

* Ep. 459 note.

438 (VIII. lxxi)

Four silver pounds, two Christmases ago,
You sent me, Postumianus, as you know.
Gifts should stand still or rise; I hoped for more;
Mine sank to half of what it was before.
The third and fourth years were below the first;
Then came one pound, a pound too of the worst.
An eight-ounce dish the sixth year's post did bear,
The seventh a cup, a poor half-pound affair.
The eighth a spoon of some two ounces weight,
The ninth an egg-spoon not a needle's freight.
Such arrant meanness would be hard to match:
With four new pounds begin another batch.

439 (VIII. lxxv)

From the Flaminian Way and Covered Road*
A poor Lingonian † to his hired abode
His way was groping, when he stubbed his toe,
His ankle twisted, and lay prostrate so.
What should he do, how stir his stranded hulk?
One tiny page-boy watched his giant bulk,—
So wizened, scarce the tiniest cloak he'ld wear;
Kind chance stepped in her timely aid to bear.
There passed, with escort of four branded slaves,
One of the thousand doomed to nameless graves.
With whispered humbleness he begged a lift;
Go where they would, 'twould answer for a shift.
Dropping their charge they toilsomely uprear
The bulging burden on the scanty bier.
So, Lucan, I have often heard it said
Of maimed Galatian, "The Gaul is dead."

* The great north road and a branch inside Rome.
† Name of a tribe in Gaul.

440 (VIII. lxxvi)

"Tell me the naked truth, dear Marcus, pray:
There's nothing I would rather hear you say."
This, when your paltry poems you are reading,
Is still your prayer, or when in court you're pleading.
It is your old importunate petition;
Hard not to grant your simple suit admission.
If you would have the naked truth, 'tis here—
But you won't like it, Gallicus, I fear.

441 (VIII. lxxviii)

PAGEANTS, ETC., IN HONOUR OF DACIAN SUCCESSES

Shows that would grace the conquering Hercules
Or Indian Bacchus with his train are these.
Joy-gifts of Stella for the North subdued,
He thinks them little, 'tis ingratitude.
Little is turbid Haemus' golden sand
Or Tagus murmuring in the western land?
For every day its gifts, the healing shower
Pours on, the commons glory in their dower.
Lo! from the clouds the merry coins rain down
And tickets for the circus flood the town,
While birds in quiet cage, from danger free,
For their new masters draw contentedly
Why tell the cars, the thirty prizes rare?
Two consuls hardly such expense could bear.
But all this pales before the consummation
That Caesar witnesses his own ovation.

442 (VIII. lxxix)

The friends that old Fabulla owns
Are harridans and ancient crones,
Ill-favoured witches, what you will;
These are her constant comrades still
To banquets, theatres, and shows;
So ever fair and young she goes.

443 (VIII. lxxxi)

Not by old Cybele's mystic shrine,
Egyptian heifer's bull* divine,

* Osiris, the bridegroom of Isis.

Or any god or goddess fair,
But by her pearls will Gellia swear.
These she'll embrace, with kisses smother,
Dearer than children, sister, brother.
Poor thing! if mischief should befall
Her pets, she could not live at all.
Papirianus, now 'tis plain
We want Serenus * back again.

* A noted burglar.

444 (VIII. lxxxii)

Caesar, beleaguered by the selfish throng,
Accept this little tribute of my song.
For letters and affairs alike you've leisure,
We know; this humble wreath may give you pleasure.
Bear with your bard; we are your glory bright,
Your chiefest care and intimate delight.
You love not oak alone but Phoebus' bays:
Take then the civic garland of my lays.

445 (IX. i)

While Janus brings us frost, Domitian * grain,
While August sees the scorching summer reign;
And while September's Kalends, day divine,
Give Caesar glory from the conquered Rhine:
While stands the rock of Rome's Tarpeian lord
And matrons throng to Julia, name adored,
While sun and starlight yet are ours, your race
Shall here be worshipped, heaven your labours grace.

* This name was given to the month October, while September was
named Germanicus, as August had been named after Augustus.

446 (IX. iii)

If you should sue the gods for all you've lent
And send your little claim for settlement,
Suppose an auction in Olympus hall
And all the powers obliged to sell their all,
Atlas* would break, and to defray the bill
Jove would not have one farthing in his till.
How to repay you for each princely shrine
And solemn rite of oak Capitoline†?
How shall great Juno pay for temples two?
I pass by Pallas; she's in league with you;
Alcides, Phoebus, Leda's children spare,
And Flavian shrines, new scope for Roman prayer‡.
Caesar, you must withhold, not push your claim;
To meet it Jove's no penny to his name.

* Who bore the heavens on his shoulders.
† When a wreath of oak-leaves was dedicated to Jupiter on the Capitol.
‡ The gods of his own family might naturally be spared contributions.

447 (IX. vii)

When, Afer, you returned from Libya home,
Five times I sought to welcome you to Rome.
"He's busy, he sleeps," five times I heard and fled:
You want no welcome: well, good-bye instead.

448 (IX. ix)

Fabius has left you nothing, as I hear,
To whom you gave six thousand year by year.
And yet, Bithynicus, you can't complain,
He will not trouble you for gifts again.

449 (IX. xi)

Name sweet as rose when violets appear
In the fresh prime and blossom of the year,
Such Hybla to the taste or Attic flowers,
Such fragrant hoard the phoenix nest embowers;
Sweeter than nectar, name for Attis meet
Or Ganymede, Jove's faithful henchman sweet,
Sound but that name within the palace hall,
Each Love and Venus answers to the call.
Fain would I write that name in dainty lay,
But one grim syllable still bars the way.
Yet poets write Eiarinos and the Greek
Unwhipt of "Ares and Ares" can speak.
But we who only write in solemn sense
Cannot aspire to such free eloquence.

450 (IX. xii)

ON THE ABOVE NAME, WHICH SIGNIFIES "CHILD OF
SPRING"

Oporinos is name for autumn's child,
Chimerinos is born in winter wild;
For summer's namesake Therinos they say;
What is he called who's born in merry May?

451 (IX. xiii)

The same.

Your name recalls the budding season gay
When bees take toll of the brief Attic May;
That name from Cytherea's* pen might be,
Or text of Acidalian* broidery;

* A name and epithet of Venus.

A name of orient pearl from eastern water,
Perfumed with amber by the sun-god's daughter.
The cranes should bear it in their merry race;
In Caesar's royal hall it should have place.

452 (IX. xiv)

This fellow, wooed by greed your friend to be,
 Think'st thou that he'll be loyal to the last?
Mullet he loves, shell, oyster, boar, not thee.
 Supped I as well, he'ld be my friend as fast.

453 (IX. xv)

Chloe seven husbands had deprived of life
 And on each tombstone to their memory
"My handiwork," she wrote. O wicked wife
 O sweet simplicity!

454 (IX. xvii)

Apollo's child*, that woo'st unwilling Fate
With sovereign herbs to lengthen mortals' date,
These precious ringlets for a granted prayer
Thy boy presents from Rome, an offering fair,
With these a mirror, whose reflected ray
Could without guile his cheerful look portray.
Cherish his youthful flower, that no less fair
He may appear with shorn than clustering hair

* Aesculapius.

455 (IX. xviii)

A PETITION FOR WATER FROM AN AQUEDUCT

Caesar, long live to bless my country home,
My little farm and tiny cote at Rome.
A crazy wheel by slow not easy stages
From shallow vale my garden's thirst assuages.
My courts no salutary fountains cheer,
Although the Marcian conduit plashes near.
Blest with thy waters, Caesar, let me dwell,
'Twill be Jove's fountain or Castalia's well.

456 (IX. xx)

This marble mansion rich with gold array
Beheld our glorious sovereign's natal day.
O happy house to hear his infant calls
And feel his feeble hands about your walls.
Here stood the stately home, that gave to earth
Like Rhodes or pious Crete a heavenly birth.
The priests hid Jupiter with clashing shield
Such as unwarlike Phrygian hand might wield.
To you the father of the gods was near;
His bolt and aegis were your shield and spear.

457 (IX. xxii)

Pastor, perhaps you'll think I ask for pelf,
Like the thick-headed vulgar, for itself;
That Setine vineyard hoe of mine may soil,
My Tuscan farm re-echo bondsmen's toil;
That ivory pillars may my board uphold,
My couches rustle in a robe of gold,

That only crystal glass my lips may touch,
And my dark wine the snowy filter smutch;
That wool-clad Tyrians may my litter bear
And bright-robed clients throng around my chair;
That page of mine may fire a tipsy guest
Nor fear with Ganymede to stand the test;
That mule may splash my robe of Tyrian grain,
Or steed obey me without spur or rein,
I ask not that. As truly as I live,
Pastor, I only ask to build and give.

458 (IX. xxiii)

Carus, late victor crowned with wreath of gold,
Where is the prize that did thy brow enfold?
"You see our sovereign's gleaming marble face;
It gave itself that noble head to grace."
The oak of olives well may jealous be,
That circled first the brows of majesty.

459 (IX. xxvi)

TO NERVA

Who poems send to please your wit divine,
Would send to Cosmos* oil of celandine,
Violets and privet white for Paestum's fee,
Corsican honey to the Hybla bee;
But yet my humble verses you may like;
Olives are not disdained, with lordly pike.
Yet, my good lord, let it not strange appear
That my poor efforts dread your critic ear.
Nero† faced not your censure undismayed,
When with light airs his youthful fancy played.

* The perfumer.
† Nerva is compared with Tibullus. Ep. 437. Nero's style was florid.

460 (IX. xxix)

Philaenis, ancient crone and Nestor's heir,
How soon you cross the dismal Stygian mere!
Scarce had you reached the Euboean Sibyl's date;
Give you some three months more, you were her mate.
Ah! what a tongue is hushed. The cry's less loud
Of busy slave-mart or Sarapis'* crowd:
Less shrill the curly-headed schoolboys' strain
Of mornings or on Strymon's banks the crane.
Who else can draw the moon with magic wheel,
Or bring for gain a wandering lord to heel?
Press on her lightly, Earth; if you're too hard,
I fear the dogs may find their purpose barred.

* The Egyptian god who took the place of Osiris at Rome.

461 (IX. xxx)

Antistius perished on the cruel shores
    Of Cappadocia*, land of guilt and dread.
Nigrina brings the ashes she adores
    And grieves her pilgrimage so soon is sped:
With sighs consigned them to the sacred mound,
And once again herself a widow found.

* A province noted for crime.

462 (IX. xxxi)

Velius, afield in Caesar's northern wars,
For safe return had vowed a goose to Mars,
Within eight courses of the circling moon
The war-god heard and claimed the promised boon.
The goose was glad to suffer for her king
And gave her life, a humble offering.

Her open beak on prey suspended gapes;
Eight coins* her body held, and these the shapes.
This bloodless tribute, Caesar, makes it plain
There is no need to draw the sword again.

* Supposed to be an omen of the eight months' campaign.

463 (IX. xxxv)

Your shame your dinner, Philomusus, buys,
For gospel truth you vouch a pack of lies.
You know of Eastern Pacorus'* last intrigue,
Can count the German or Sarmatian league,
By you each Dacian secret is revealed,
Your prescience scents each victory ere sealed.
You know what rains on dark Syene† pour,
What ships have started from the Libyan shore,
For whose imperial head the olives‡ shine,
To whom the Father§ will his wreath resign.
A truce to this; you'll dine with me to-day,
You're welcome, but we'll have no gossip, pray.

* A Parthian king.
† The southern boundary of Egypt.
‡ The crown at the games of the Quinquatrus, given by the emperor.
§ Jupiter's oak-wreath at the Capitoline Games.

464 (IX. xxxviii)

THE CONJURER

Swift Agathinus, daring to the end,
You will not drop the shield, as you pretend.
Cast off, your flight it follows through the air,
Then lights on foot or back or nail or hair.
What though the stage be wet with saffron spray
And furious winds the anchored awning sway?

Unheeded still the artist it pursues,
Though wind and water their consent refuse.
Trip as you will, when you have done your all
It cleaves. It would be cleverer still to fall.

465 (IX. xliii)

ON A STATUETTE OF HERCULES

This great bronze god upon a lion's hide
For ease from galling rock, a covering wide,
Gazing upon the heavens he once bore up,
In his left hand a club, his right a cup,
Is no new work of Roman quality,
But famed Lysippus'* plastic artistry.
It graced the Macedonian hero's feast,
The darkened meteor of the conquered East.
By this young Hannibal swore vengeance dire;
This bade fell Sulla from his task retire.
Loathing the tyrannous court's caprice and pride
In humbler dwelling now it fain would bide.
Of kind Molorchus † 'twas of old the guest,
And now with learned Vindex deigns to rest.

* Sculptor of Alexander the Great.
† A peasant who entertained Hercules, who made him rich.

466 (IX. xlv)

Once, Marcellinus, 'neath the sluggish Wain*
And Getic stars thy frozen path has lain,
Now to the rock-bed of Prometheus † go
And gaze, young soldier, on a Titan's woe.

* The northern stars appear to move more slowly than the southern.
† Prometheus made the first man, and for his benefit stole fire from
   heaven, for which Zeus tortured but could not kill him.

When you behold our benefactor's cliff
Sighing you'll say, "He was himself more stiff."
And you may add, "Who braved the savage rock,
Might well be father of the human stock."

467 (IX. xlvi)

Gellius is building; threshold he must set,
Or bolts and bars to keep the doorway get,
Or windows want repairing and renewing,
Let him but build, no matter what he's doing.
So, when a friend asks money by and by,
"I'm sorry, but I'm building," he'll reply.

468 (IX. xlviii)

A LEGACY-HUNTER'S TROUBLES

You'd left me just a fourth part of your store,
By all that's sacred, Garricus, you swore.
I own, it tempted me, for hope is pleasant,
And so I fostered mine with many a present.
Among them was a boar Laurentine bred:
You'ld think in Calydon* its course was sped.
You asked both lords and commons, each his fill
Was promised; Rome has indigestion still.
Even I myself was there, nor meanly placed,
Yet not a rib nor tail my platter graced.
All hope of my fourth share I must renounce,
Of my own boar I'd not a single ounce.

* Scene of the fatal boar-hunt of Meleager. Ep. 246.

469 (IX. xlix)

This is the toga* famed in many a lay,
Which countless readers know and love to-day.
A poet's memorable gift, it bore
Your name, Parthenius; this my knighthood† wore
Conspicuous, while its dainty web might claim
A lustre worthy of the giver's name‡.
Now it is old, for tottering pauper fit,
A snowy toga, you may vouch for it§.
How the fell hand of passing years we see!
Once for Parthenius, now 'tis meet for me.

* Ep. 407.   † Ep. 224.
‡ Parthenius means "virgin-like."
§ As cold as snow, if not as white.

470 (IX. l)

But little, Gaurus, you account my wit,
Because with brevity I season it.
Quite true, and you, who of old Priam prate
Through twelve long books, are to be reckoned great.
I make a dwarf of living flesh and blood,
You, great one, make a giant, but of mud.

471 (IX. li)

Lucan, against your brother's will you prayed
To die before him. Death your will obeyed.
Tho' later born, Tullus like hope had nursed,
And envied you your lot in passing first.
You, in Elysium dwelling, who before
Sighed for his presence, sigh for it no more.
Castor for his dead brother left the sky:
If you were Pollux, Castor should not die.

472 (IX. lii)

Believe me, dearest Ovid, when I say
That as mine own I love your natal day.
March first and first of April, names how bright,
Meet to be marked with stones of purest white.
The former gave me birth, but this a friend;
The greater blessing did your month attend.

473 (IX. liv)

FEBRUARY GIFTS TO KINSMEN

Had I fat fieldfare blanched in olive oil,
Did Sabine woodland spread my wily toil,
My tapered reed its finny quarry play
Or sticky birdlime trap my feathered prey,
These gifts would kinship, Carus, send to thee:
Nor brother, grandsire dearer were to me.
Here paltry starlings and poor finches sing,
And the pert sparrows chirrup to the spring.
Here to the jay the ditcher makes reply,
While yonder pilfering hawk ascends the sky.
Take from my chicken-yard this offering small;
Be gracious, and we'll often cousins call.

474 (IX. lv)

On Cousins' Day, with fieldfares in the air,
Both you and Stella would have had your share,
But there's a hitch; the crowd I might offend,
Each one of whom is my particular friend.
Two to oblige were sweet; to offend the many
Were dangerous, to feed would cost a penny.
Forgive me; it's the only thing to do:
Send none to Stella, Flaccus*, none to you.

* Ep. 37.

475 (IX. lviii)

A DEDICATION

>Queen of the sacred pool, sweet Nymph divine,
>To whom Sabinus gives a grateful shrine,
>A joy for ever, so may Umbria love you
>Nor Sassina* rate the Baian waves above you,
>Accept my anxious verse with kindly smile;
>You'll be my Hippocrene spring the while.
>"Who to the Nymphs their verses dedicate
>Give a shrewd forecast of their destined fate†."

>   * Where the fountain was.   † A cold bath.

476 (IX. lix)

A DAY'S SHOPPING

>Mamurra, long a wanderer through the store
>Where golden Rome turns her vast treasures o'er,
>The dainty slaves devoured with greedy eye,
>Not common lads of vulgar quality,
>But boys select, the dealer's choicest crew,
>Fit for the rich, unmeet for me and you.
>Sated, he stripped the covered tables bare
>And asked to see the piles of ivory rare.
>Thinking a sofa, tortoiseshell, to buy
>He measured it four times. "Too small," he'ld sigh.
>He asked his nose if Corinth bronze were true
>And, Polyclitus, found great fault with you.
>The crystal glass was badly flawed, he'ld say,
>Yet marked ten cups and stowed them safe away.
>He weighed old goblets, if they struck his taste
>As by the handiwork of Mentor graced.

Emeralds set in gold he counted o'er
And rattling earrings from the dealer's store.
At every table sardonyx he sought,
Knew at what price great jaspers should be bought.
Worn out at five, at last he homeward hies;
Bearing two halfpenny mugs, his only prize.

477 (IX. lx)

Fresh wreath from Tusculum now blushing red,
From Paestum or from Tibur's rosy bed,
Or were you some Praenestine gardener's pride,
Or jewel of Campania's country side?
That to Sabinus you may smell more sweet,
Say that you come from my Laurentine seat.

478 (IX. lxi)

THE PLANE-TREE OF JULIUS CAESAR

There stands a far-famed house in Spanish land
Where wealthy Corduba loves calm Baetis' strand,
Where yellow fleeces glow with native gold
And living foil o'erfilms the western fold.
O'ershadowing all the roof with mantle green
Of thickest foliage, Caesar's plane is seen.
The conquering hand that planted luckily
Charmed the young rod into a lofty tree.
Proud of its lord, his tender nursling fair
Burgeoned and tossed great limbs in upper air.
The tipsy Fauns beneath its shadow played;
Oft their late pipe the silent home dismayed.
At night the Dryad through the country side
Flying from Pan beneath its leaves would hide.

Perfumed by revelling Bacchus all the place
Smelt sweet. His wine-cups swelled the tree apace.
Yesterday's ruddy leaves all round were thrown,
Relics of chaplets none might call his own.
O happy day, O mighty Caesar's tree,
Fear not the axe, the hearth's impiety!
Year after year your honours you'll renew,
For 'twas no Pompey's hand that planted you.

479 (IX. lxiv)

Caesar stoops low. He's Hercules * to-day
And gives new temples to the Latin way,
Where travellers seeking Trivia's woodland home
Mark the eighth milestone on the road from Rome.
Once wooed with prayer and blood, now out of date,
The less Alcides worships now the great.
To him the suitor turns for wealth or place,
To the other they appeal for lesser grace.
 * Ep. 505.

480 (IX. lxviii)

What quarrel, pedagogue, hast thou with me,
That art of lad and lass the enemy?
Ere crested chanticleer salutes the day
With thundering growl and scourge you peg away.
So noisy hammers upon anvils beat
The lawyer on his copper horse to seat.
Less fierce and fell thunders the crowd's applause
To hail the victor than your savage tawse.
We neighbours ask not sleep the livelong night,
To wake is nothing; not to sleep's the plight.
Dismiss your harried troop; your chattering cease.
What are your fees? Take them to hold your peace.

481 (IX. lxx)

"Fie on the age," was Tully's broken cry
When Catilina's impious hopes ran high,
When son and father clashed in civil strife
And all the land ran red with squandered life.
But wherefore cry you "Fie for shame" to-day,
Caecilianus? Where's the grievance, pray?
We have no savage chiefs, no mad distress,
We bask in peace and settled happiness.
Your vision shows you faults in every class;
'Tis your own character that dims the glass.

482 (IX. lxxi)

Here is indeed a miracle to see,
Lion and ram in loving harmony.
Go up yourself and look. One stall they share,
Partake one common life, one common fare.
Together not on grass or leaves they feed,
A gentle lamb must for their table bleed.
What were the Nemean scourge*, Phrixus' false guide†,
That they should shine as stars beatified?
If for dumb creatures there's a heaven assigned,
Then these two friends deserve such grace to find.

* The lion killed by Hercules.
† The ram that dropped Helle in the sea.

483 (IX. lxxii)

Liber, great champion of the boxing ring,
Our thews to Grecian art apprenticing,
You send a luncheon basket. Why, I ask,
Why comes it widowed of its faithful flask?

Had you a gift to suit your name* invented,
Your jolly godsire would be represented.

* Liber is the same as Bacchus the god of wine.

484 (IX. lxxiii)

A COBBLER TURNED SQUIRE

Wont with your teeth to gnaw an ancient hide,
Mumble the filthy sole and stretch it wide,
Your patron's trust abused, a home you find
In fair Praeneste, once its worthless hind*.
My silly parents taught me A, B, C,
And what have grammar, rhetoric done for me?
Thalia, leave your books and take an awl,
If such a prize can to a cobbler fall.

* He was cobbler to the estate (a slave's position).

485 (IX. lxxiv)

Camonus' father had his infant face
Portrayed. The childish image keeps its place.
No likeness of his prime the father drew,
He could not bear those silent lips to view.

486 (IX. lxxv)

Tucca's cold bath is not of concrete thick,
Basaltic rock or Babylonian brick.
'Tis all compact of timber, pine and lath;
Tucca might go a-sailing in his bath.
The fellow's rich; a hot bath too he made
Of mottled marble rich with every shade,
Phrygian and African and Spartan too;
If firewood fails, the swimming-bath will do.

487 (IX. lxxvi)

Camonus, whom the artist here portrays,
Such form and feature showed in early days.
Now strengthening time had doubled ten years' space
And Nature, smiling, sketched a bearded face,
This glossy hair had fallen before the knife,
When one fell Sister grudged his tender life,
With hasty hand his thread too quickly shore
And left his father ashes, nothing more.
Then, lest his childhood live by art alone,
His manhood's image in my verse be shown.

488 (IX. lxxviii)

Your Galla's buried seven: 'twas time the shrew
Died, Picentinus; so she married you.

489 (IX. lxxxi)

Reader and hearer, Aulus, love my stuff;
A certain poet says it's rather rough.
Well, I don't care. For dinners or for books
The guest's opinion matters, not the cook's.

490 (IX. lxxxii)

A prophet read your fortune in the sky
"A bier untimely." Munna, 'twas no lie.
Fearing you might leave something after you,
With reckless waste you ran your fortune through.
Your two whole million fled in scarce a year.
What else is meant by "an untimely bier"?

491 (IX. lxxxiii)

A TRUCE TO RECITATION

Caesar, for all the wonders of your show,
Surpassing all the pomp of long ago,
Our ears are more indebted than our sight.
Our bards are silent while they watch the fight.

492 (IX. lxxxiv)

Norbanus, while your constant honour, tried
In Caesar's battles, rebel rage defied,
Snug in the shelter of the Muses' shade
Your ancient friend and crony still I played.
My verse by every Rhaetian* was quoted,
My fame by every Vindelician* noted.
How often, faithful to old friendship's name,
"My poet, he's my poet," you'll exclaim.
All this, for twice six summers known by sound,
Its author sends you for your reading bound.

* Tribes near the German border subject to Rome.

493 (IX. lxxxv)

A DINNER INVITATION CANCELLED

Atilius, when our Paulus "loses tone,"
He spares his friends' digestion, not his own.
Your sudden illness for a freak you plead,
But my poor dinner is a corpse indeed.

494 (IX. lxxxvii)

After seven cups of drink divine,
Lips, tongue and brain afloat in wine,

You bring me certain drafts to read;
"Nasta, my father's slave, I've freed;
Pray sign and seal." Some time I may;
I only seal the flask to-day.

495 (IX. lxxxviii)

You overlaid your hook with gifts galore;
You caught me, Rufus, and sent gifts no more.
To keep your prey the creature must be fed.
The hungry boar will vanish from his shed.

496 (IX. lxxxix)

Stella, you're downright hard upon your guest.
"Write verse," you say. Well, do not ask my best

497 (IX. xc)

So on some spangled meadow may you lie
Lulled by the shimmering rivulet's melody
Of pebbles by the rounded wavelets stirred,
All business and all carking care deferred,
And strain through cooling snow the vintage rare,
With ruddy garlands twined about your hair;
Shun Cyprus, Flaccus*, I implore, entreat,
Cyprus, that cauldron of Levantine heat,
What time your floor with rustling sheaves is piled
And in the welkin glares the Lion wild.
Kind Venus, send my brother back to me,
So may thy Martian Kalends worship thee,
Unscathed; and so let incense, blood and wine
And square of cake be offered at thy shrine.

* Ep. 37.

498 (IX. xciii)

Crown, crown the bowl: put two-fold measure in
Of good Falernian from the ancient bin.
Say, to what godhead, Calocissus, flow
Six brimming measures? Caesar's name they show*.
Ten times let fragrant wreaths your hair embrace
For him whose temples shrine his noble race†.
Now with ten kisses you shall answer me
For the great conqueror of the Odrysae‡.

* One measure for each letter is the rule for toasts.
† Domitianus.
‡ Perhaps Germanicus, another title of Domitian.

499 (IX. xciv)

UNEQUAL INTERCHANGE OF GIFTS

Hippocrates, of shame you give no sign,
Wormwood to send, and ask for honeyed wine.
Glaucus* was wiser in brave days of old
Who gave for bronze his panoply of gold.
Your bitter you would have for sweet exchanged?
Drink it in hellebore†; your mind's deranged.

* Who exchanged his golden armour for Diomedes' bronze.
† The drink prescribed for madness.

500 (IX. xcvi)

A THIEF'S EXCUSE. HEROD WAS A PHYSICIAN

From his sick friend Herod the cup withdrew,
Caught, he exclaimed, "Drinking's so bad for you."

501 (IX. xcvii)

He bursts with spite (dear coz, you know the wight!)
That Rome admires my verse, he bursts with spite.
He bursts with spite that in the public sight
Each finger points me out, he bursts with spite.
He bursts with spite, for that full citizen right*
Two Caesars granted me, he bursts with spite!
He bursts with spite that town and suburbs bright
Both have snug homes for me, he bursts with spite!
He bursts with spite that courteous hosts invite
And true friends cherish me, he bursts with spite!
He bursts with spite that love and praise unite.
So burst, so curst be all who burst with spite.

* Properly given to the father of three children but granted to Martial, see Ep. 108.

502 (IX. xcviii)

On the same subject as Epp. 146–7.

The vintage, Ovid, by the rain
Has realized a local gain:
Coranus made his empty bin
A place for putting water in.

503 (IX. xcix)

Marcus Antonius* loves my verses well,
If truth, my Atticus, his letters tell,
Marcus, Tolosa's literary child,
Born in the age of peaceful quiet mild.
Book, thou art fit the weary way to wend,
Go as a keepsake from an absent friend:

* M. Antonius Primus the former general and agent of Vespasian.

A gift of little price, if that were all;
For you the interest is personal.
A stream is sweeter at the source, I trow,
Than in the dull and lifeless pool below.

504 (IX. c)

For half-a-crown* you bid me through the dew
Each morning, Bassus, pay my court to you,
Cleave to your side, accompany your chair
And call upon old women everywhere.
My gown† is coarse and cheap and old, I fear;
Yet half-a-crown for it were scarcely dear.

* The client's dole at each visit.
† The necessary toga.

505 (IX. ci)

DOMITIAN POSED AS A "GREATER HERCULES," AND
REPLACED HERCULES' STATUE BY HIS OWN

Compare Ep. 479.

Immortal Appius, upon whose road*
Our sovereign Hercules new fame bestowed,
Would you his predecessor's worth compute,
He felled Antaeus, won the golden fruit,
The warrior maiden's girdle bore away,
The boar and lion flayed, foul birds from day
Cut off, from woods the brazen-footed deer,
And dragged the monster from the Stygian mere,
The Hydra's issue dried, that grew with slaughter,
And bathed his western herd in Tiber's water.
Thus far the less; now of the greater learn,
Whose altar-lamps by the sixth milestone burn.

* The great southern road.

The oppressor from the seat of power he threw*
And sovereign Jove his young defender knew.
Sole lord, Iulus'† mantle he laid down,
Third ruler in a world late all his own.
Three times he crushed the treacherous Danube's pride
And bathed his charger in its snow-fed tide.
Thrifty of triumphs, yet he won a name,
And from the northern world a conqueror came.
Shrines to the gods he gave and rest from wars,
To his folk virtue, fame to his own, new stars
To heaven; for Hercules a rôle too great,
That rather might beseem the Thunderer's state.

* In Vespasian's absence, Domitian as his deputy secured the Palatine
and Capitol.
† The son and (for a brief space) deputy of Aeneas, as Domitian of
Vespasian.

506 (IX. cii)

You send me, receipted, your little account;
Four hundred, I think, is the proper amount.
Such benefit, Phoebus, scarce makes me your debtor,
A loan of a hundred would suit me much better.
Your debt was past hope ere you signed it away;
'Tis no thanks to you that I've nothing to pay.

507 (X. i)

Should my long-windedness awake alarm,
A little of me at a time won't harm.
Some epigrams are in a page compressed;
So, if you want me shorter, skip the rest.

508 (x. ii)

This, my tenth volume, sped unmarked astray*,
But 'tis revised and overhauled to-day.
Familiar matter in new dress you'll find,
But more that's new. To either verse be kind,
Reader, my treasure; Rome can tell how dear,
Who gave thee, saying, "Take my best; 'tis here;
By him ungrateful Lethe thou shalt flee
And thy best part have immortality."
The fig-tree splits Messala's† marble blocks,
And the rough drover draggled Crispus† mocks.
Verses grow great with Time and Fate defy;
Such monuments alone can never die.

* An edition had been published in haste.
† Nobles whose monuments were extant but injured.

509 (x. iii)

Slang of the footlights, envy's bitter juice,
Obscene epitome of tramps' abuse
That for a match's value would not pass
With vendor of dilapidated glass,
Some hole-and-corner poet up and down
Scatters as mine, Priscus, about the town.
Say, would you hear a squawking parrot's rail
For the melodious music of the quail?
Shall Canus play the bag-pipe? Far from me
Be this invention of the enemy.
My fame soars high; why should it stoop and fall,
When to be silent is no cost at all?

510 (X. iv)

You read of Oedipus, Thyestes' feast,
Colchis and Scylla and each fabled beast.
Hylas, Parthenopaeus and their crew,
Endymion, Attis, what are they to you?
What the poor boy stripped of his gliding wings,
Or he who bathed in the amatory springs?
For lying fables why such deep concern?
To life's realities, Mamurra, turn.
No Centaur, Gorgon, Harpy here you'll see,
But the brief abstract of humanity.
Your self, your character, you do not heed?
If so, Mamurra, you may Aetia* read.

* Or Origins, by Callimachus, then popular.

511 (X. v)

ON THE WRITER OF A SCURRILOUS POEM IN MARTIAL'S NAME

Whoe'er it was who durst in honour's spite
Of stole and purple scurril treason write,
Let him an outcast be of bridge and hill
And, meanest of our squalid beggars, still
Beg scraps of filthy offal. On him beat,
Bereft of shelter, long December's sleet.
Let him cry, "Blest indeed, thrice happy they,
Who in the death-god's chariot take their way."
May dogs behowl him as his last hour drags,
Scaring the carrion birds with fluttered rags.
May death itself his horrid doom prolong,
Pursued by Aeacus' relentless throng,

Crushed by the rock of Sisyphus the shifty,
Or in the gossip's* pond athirst, till, fifty
Old nightmares crowding at the Fury's sign,
He conscience-stricken own "The verse was mine."

* Tantalus, punished for telling tales.

512 (x. vi)

TRAJAN

Happy their chance, who view our chief returning
With northern suns and planets round him burning.
When comes the promised dawn, when field and tree
And windows flash with bright-eyed galaxy?
The expectant pause, the far-off dusty cloud,
The northern road clogged by a jostling crowd?
When will the knights and Moors with broidered gear
Ride forth amid the general shout, "He's here"?

513 (x. vii)

Rhine, father of each Nymph and stream that owes
Its foster-cradle to Odrysian snows,
So be thy current ever clear nor feel
The savage herdsman's rude and trampling wheel:
So may thy golden horns be raised once more,
So Roman be thy course from shore to shore,
Give Trajan back; a loyal empire needs
His coming, and thy sovereign Tiber pleads.

514 (x. viii)

Paula's rich and fifty-five,
    Paula's love, I scout it.
Were she sixty, as I live,
    I would think about it.

515 (x. ix)

TO HIMSELF

Martial, renowned throughout the world's domain,
The moral jester in Catullus' vein,
There is small ground for envy at thy star;
The horse Andraemon is more famed by far.

516 (x. x)

THE STRUGGLE FOR PATRONAGE

When you, whose brows the laurel wreaths adorn,
Beset a thousand thresholds every morn,
What shall I do? Paulus, what's left to me,
A man of common, vulgar quality?
I call my patron lord and master too;
The same, how much more daintily, do you.
I wait on chair or litter, you take hire
Yourself and fight for passage through the mire.
I rise when he recites; amazed you stand
And blow him favouring kisses with each hand.
God help the would-be client if he's poor!
Your purple robes have shown our gowns the door.

518 (x. xv)

"Aper's killed his wife, sir."
      "Rich by all report?"
"'Twas in sport he shot her."
      Gad! what splendid sport!

519 (x. xvi)

Gaius, a promise is a gift, you say:
I'll beat you with my bounteous gifts to-day.
Take all the treasure of Asturian mines,
And gold that in the sand of Tagus shines,

Of Orient pearls by negroes won the best
And all the treasure of the Phoenix' nest,
The choice of rascal Tyre's empurpled sea:
Take all the world, even as you give it me.

520 (x. xvii)

You would rob Macer of his Christmas prize;
You can't, my man; he asks, if one denies.
He claims my yearly crop, my merry lay,
And grumbles that my Muse is mute to-day.
Now for his pay-sheets only he has time.
Poor Appian road *, if he must read my rhyme!

* Of which Macer was surveyor.

521 (x. xviii)

Marius won't ask you or send gifts to you,
Go bail or lend; but then he's not a sou.
Yet he's a crowd their barren friend to bleed.
Alas! Poor Rome's a silly fool indeed.

522 (x. xix)

Go, Muse, to eloquent Pliny bear my verse;
Not wise, not over strict, it might be worse.
To scale Suburra's but a small affair;
Right up the steep you go and you are there.
There dizzy Orpheus tunes his magic string
Above the Coliseum's dabbled ring;
The wondering beasts and that celestial bird
Behold who Ganymede to heaven transferred;
Here too an eagle, but of lowlier flight,
Seems on thy Pedo's modest porch to light.

But of an alien hour beware, my rhyme,
Nor, drunken, trespass on a scholar's time.
Whole days he spends upon a wise oration
Meet for the Hundred Judges' approbation,
That future unborn ages may compare
With Arpine Cicero's immortal ware.
Go to him late by lamplight. Better so,
When all the house with Bacchus is aglow,
When roses reign and fragrant spices bleed;
Then rugged Cato's self my verse would read.

523 (X. xx)

If I would see the golden Salo's shore
And my loved eagle's nest in Spain once more,
You, Manius, from my early boyhood dear,
Old friend and playmate of my fifteenth year,
You are the cause. In all my native ground
None sweeter, none more worthy love is found.
With you the thirsty Libyan's hut I'ld know
Or share the tent-mat of the Scythian foe.
You feel with me, to your old friend you're true?
The desert will be Rome for me and you.

524 (X. xxi)

Why, Sextus, do you love to write such stuff
As skilled grammarians would find hard and tough?
You want no reader, but interpreter.
Cinna to the great Mantuan* you prefer.
Well, wear your bays: I'll ne'er a scholar flout,
Though scholar's sanction I can do without.
* Virgil.

525 (X. xxiii)

Thrice five Olympiads in a green old age
Kind Primus* numbers for his heritage.
Reviewing all his gentle life-time o'er
He has no fear of Lethe's nearing shore.
The day was never tedious nor unkind,
Or, passing, left a canker in the mind.
The good man lengthens out his earthly skein,
For living in the past is life again.

* M. Antonius, Ep. 503.

526 (X. xxiv)

First of March, when I was born,
Fairer than each opening morn,
When the girls send gifts to me,
Seven and fifty cakes shall be
On my hearth with incense fine.
Add to these but nine and nine,
That not yet with years o'ercast
I may reach my goal at last.
Give me twenty-five times three,
After, not a day for me.

527 (X. xxv)

Mucius—you saw him in the circus stand
And in the blazing censer plunge his hand—
If he seems stout and stubborn to endure,
You have the wit of an Abderite boor.
When, under pain of fiery doom, they say
"Burn off your hand," 'tis easier to obey.

528 (x. xxvi)

Varus, in Egypt's cities famed afar,
Known to thy hundred as a man of war,
Ah! vainly promised to thy native land,
Thy ashes rest on the Lagean* strand.
We might not shed a tributary tear
Nor sorrowing pour fat incense on thy bier.
But lasting name is given thee by the Muse;
This offering treacherous Nile thou'lt not refuse.

* Egyptian, so called after Lagus the ancestor of the Ptolemies.

529 (x. xxvii)

A PARVENU

For the idea compare Ep. 103, note.

Your birthday, Diodorus, sees a horde
Of Knights and Senators about your board.
Your fasting client thirty pence* receives;
Yet in your birth no single soul believes.

* More than usual.

530 (x. xxviii)

Father of years, sire of the heavens so fair,
First greeted of the gods by Roman prayer,
Of old you kept a dainty house and small
In the mid traffic's roaring carnival.
Now Caesar's lavish gift your threshold graces,
And every front looks out on pillared spaces.
If, Janus, grateful for such boons you'ld be,
Close your steel portals fast to earthly key*.

* In token of peace.

531 (X. xxx)

Formiae, to thy sweet coast and balmy airs
Apollinaris weary oft repairs
From city's feud and ever haunting care;
Best of all home he loves thy haven fair;
Not Antium or Praeneste's calm retreat,
Not Tusculum or Algidus so sweet.
Circe, Caieta, lazy Liris blue
Nor Lucrine Salmacis thy waves outdo.
A gentle breeze doth o'er the surface glide,
No idle flood; the ocean's heaving tide
Wafts with the favouring air the painted keels;
So maid's gay fan from summer freshness steals.
Alone, recumbent in his easy chair
The fisher draws his quarry by a hair.
If e'er the ocean feels the wind-god's sway,
Secure the larder laughs the storm away.
The ponds with myriad pike and turbot throng,
Tame lampreys to their master swim along.
The keeper knows each gurnard on the roll,
Grey mullets, doubly grey, obey the scroll.
When shall I, Formiae, by these toils of care
Untrammelled, in thy sweet contentment share?
O happy household, happy bailiff crew;
These joys, designed for others, slave for you.

532 (X. xxxi)

You sold a slave, some forty crowns the deal,
To purchase you a single greedy meal.
A four-pound mullet, most expensive beast,
Was the chief dainty of your cannibal feast.

Calliodorus, well may we exclaim,
"You eat a man and not a fish. For shame!"

533 (X. xxxii)

This likeness, set in violet and rose,
Whose face does it portray, do you suppose?
Even such was Marcus * in his lusty years.
In this his youth to his old eyes appears.
Caedicianus, could we paint his mind,
No fairer portrait on the earth we'ld find.

* Antonius, Ep. 503, note.

534 (X. xxxiii)

Munatius, Sabine in simplicity,
In whom a kindlier Socrates we see,
So on your child may Love's pure lustre shine
And bless your link with an illustrious line,
If verses dipped in wormwood and in gall
Perchance malicious envy mine should call,
Repel the charge as mad; stand up and say
No one would read such foul abuse to-day.
My lines have learnt to keep this measure nice,
To spare the guilty but rebuke the vice.

535 (X. xxxv)

Sulpicia's verses every wife should read,
If she would have her lord her lord indeed.
And, if he would retain a loyal bride,
Each spouse should have Sulpicia at his side.
Not mad Medea desecrates her rhyme,
Nor the foul horrors of old Atreus' crime;

No Byblis is her theme, no Scylla fell,
Of chaste and pious love her pages tell.
Of sport, delight and jollity she'll sing,
And to the test a two-fold merit bring;
Seldom such innocence and wit compete;
In her our old Egeria* we greet.
With her for guide or school-mate, Sappho's flame
Had been the brighter, nor her life to blame.
Thy peerless charms once seen and purity,
Hard-hearted Phaon had made love to thee.
In vain; for not Apollo, Bacchus, Jove,
Calenus torn from her, had won her love.
* The supposed bride of Numa.

536 (X. xxxvi)

The wine that vile Massilia's smoke-rooms stock,
Mellowed too soon, the buyer's taste to mock,
Comes from you, Munna. To your injured friends
O'er land and sea the fiery flagon wends.
And that not cheap. It costs, your filthy brand,
What Setine or Falernian could command.
I'm not surprised we never see you here;
It is your vile concoction that you fear.

537 (X. xxxvii)

BEFORE DEPARTING FOR SPAIN

Maternus, law and equity's firm stay,
Whose just pronouncement Roman courts obey,
If any message for an ancient friend
And fellow townsman you to Spain would send,
Command me. Who would waste another day
On sprats and tadpoles in Laurentum bay,

When he might fling good mullet in the foam
And carry nothing but three-pounders home?
In smooth-shelled mussels who would seek a zest
To tempt the palate of a favoured guest,
When host and household might alike partake
A dainty worthy of the Lucrine lake?
You with loud cries the noisome fox will snare
And an ignoble prey your hounds will tear;
There, dripping seines drawn from the fishy sea
Will mesh the timid hare as meat for me.
Even now your fisher owns his wasted toil,
And a poor marten is your huntsman's spoil!
The ocean waits your bidding; here at home
The shore must fatten on the scraps of Rome.

538 (x. xxxix)
NO LONGER YOUNG

"In Brutus' consulship you saw the light";
    You were born rather under Numa's sway,
Nay, that is little. If tradition's right,
    Your mould was fashioned of Promethean clay.

539 (x. xli)

At the new year your husband you disown
And, Proculeia, bid him live alone.
For what offence do you give him so the slip?
Pray hear the truth; he's gained the praetorship.
To Cybele's games * and robe his duty owes
A hundred thousand, though with scanty shows;
The public offering twenty thousand more.
You will not part, then is not parting sore.

* Paid for by the praetor of the year.

540 (x. xliii)

> Your seventh wife lies buried in your field.
> Phileros, did ever farm such harvest yield?

541 (x. xliv)

> And must you, Ovid, view the British shore,
> See Tethys green, hear father Ocean roar,
> From Numa's hills, Nomentum's comfort stray,
> Nor hearth nor furrow tempt your age to stay?
> Joys you defer, but Fate still plies her shears:
> Each passing hour against your name appears.
> To serve your friend, God bless your chivalry,
> Life is less dear than constant loyalty.
> Soon to your Sabine farm return to dwell,
> And show some friendship for yourself as well.

542 (x. xlv)

> If light and sweetness in my books there be,
> If my verse breathe of gentle courtesy,
> You say it cloys. You like a bone to eat
> And think Laurentine haunch a sorry treat.
> Drink Vatican, if vinegar you ask;
> Your appetite would turn against my flask.

543 (x. xlvi)

GOOD ADVICE

> Good Matho, prettiness enough we've had;
> Now write us something good, or something bad.

544 (x. xlvii)

TO HIS COUSIN

Dear Martial, if you'ld happy be,
Here's the unfailing recipe.
An income not procured by toil,
A blazing hearth, a grateful soil,
Quiet, undress, no suit at law,
Good health and strength without a flaw,
Shrewd frankness, many a loyal heart,
Kind guests, a table void of art,
Nights careless, sober, bed that's chaste
But cheerful, sleep the night to waste;
Contented seek no other fate,
Nor wish nor fear your death to wait.

545 (x. xlviii)

The eighth hour ended now may Isis learn*
And on their way the household troops return.
The bath-room's cooler than an hour before,
Ere that a torture, nothing less or more.
Cerealis, Nepos, Stella, Flaccus, meet
Canius and Lupus †; just enough to seat.
The farmer's wife will wholesome mallows bring
And all the treasures of her gardening.
Here's the squat lettuce and the close-cut leek,
Rocket and windy mint are not to seek;
Stewed eggs will dress sea-lizard girt with rue,
There'll be a haggis, pickled tunny too.
This for a whet. One table spreads the feast,
A kidling rescued from a savage beast,

* When the worshippers assembled.
† For the names comp. Epp. 31, 617.

Cutlets that need no carver's knife, and beans,
The workman's relish, and rough early greens.
A chicken and a ham three turns surviving,
Ripe apples presently you'll see arriving,
Wine from Nomentum without lees you'll sip,
Born in old Fronto's second consulship.
There will be stingless mirth, free speech and laughter,
Nought best unsaid or to be feared hereafter.
Of Blue and Green* our whole discourse shall be;
Our cups shall put no man in jeopardy.

* The racing colours.

546 (x. xlix)

From cups of precious amethyst you dine
And swill yourself with black Opimian wine.
Your loving-cup is with new Sabine filled:
Hence, leaden liquor! you're too base to gild.

547 (x. l)

ON THE DEATH OF A FAMOUS JOCKEY

Break victory's palms! What boots Judaea's fall?
Beat your bare breasts for grief, ye backers all!
Let Honour mourn; sad Glory, rend your hair
And cast into the flames your garland fair.
O cruel wrong, Scorpus has run his race
Too soon and yokes his funeral team apace.
So brief, so rapid was thy chariot's flight,
How sped thy day so quickly to its night!

548 (x. li)

The Bull to turn upon the Ram begins
And winter's fled before the Heavenly Twins;
Each field and tree and meadow's clothed and gay,
And Philomela tunes her doleful lay.
What happy days has Rome, Faustinus, cost you,
What lounging in Ravenna's* sunshine lost you!
O wood and rills and shore of oozing sand
And shimmering sea-girt Anxur! On each hand
Your easy couch commands two prospects free,
Ships in the river channel and the sea.
True, there no theatre salutes the Graces,
No baths appear, no gorgeous columned spaces:
You'll see no Thunderer's temple soaring high,
Nor great Vespasian's towering to the sky.
Weary, how oft to Romulus you'll say,
"Keep what is yours; give me my own, I pray."

* The name of the estate, not the town.

549 (x. liii)

The same as 547.

I'm Scorpus, glory of the shouting ring,
Rome's brief delight, her thrice applauded king,
Whom jealous Fate within six lustres' span
Counting his palms took for an aged man.

550 (x. liv)

Your table tops are good; but why not shown?
I could find covers, Olus, for my own.

F

551 (x. lvi)

Gallus, you'ld have me slave, my court to pay,
Up muddy Aventine four times a day.
Cascellius draws a grinder or repairs,
Hyginus rids the eyes of smarting hairs.
Moist ulcers fall by Fannius' bloodless hand,
Eros relieves a slave of tell-tale brand.
Hermes is good at rupture. There it ceases;
For who shall mend me if I come in pieces?

552 (x. lvii)

Once you sent a pound of silver; now but half a pound
    you send;
Half a pound of pepper, Sextus: pepper is too dear, my
    friend.

553 (x. lviii)

AN EXCUSE FOR NOT CALLING

When we, Frontinus, Anxur's peaceful view
And Baiae's homelike coast more closely knew,
To wood and lake withdrawn from Cancer's reign
And the loud cricket's unrelenting strain,
Of learned converse we could have our fill;
Here the great city keeps me at the mill.
What day's my own? Upon the town I'm tossed,
And in a barren toil my life is lost,
Rugged suburban land I feed and till
And tend my homestead by Quirinus' hill.
Friendship has other tests: 'twere shameful price
A poet's days and nights to sacrifice.
By all the powers, and that dear Muse I serve,
My heart is faithful, though attention swerve.

554 (x. lix)

You've read one epigram; the rest you skip;
Shortness, not sweetness suits your censorship.
A whole rich mart's outspread before your feet;
And yet a small tit-bit's your only treat.
I want no gluttonous reader, no, indeed!
Still I prefer one who on bread can feed.

555 (x. lx)

Munna's three pupils now: on that account he
Has claimed the benefit of Caesar's bounty*.

* Alluding to the privileges enjoyed by the *parents* of three children.
  See note on Ep. 501.

556 (x. lxi)

Here lies Erotion at untimely date,
In his sixth year cut down by cruel fate.
You, my successor in this little field,
To his poor ashes annual tribute yield.
So prosper house and home, and on this land
No other monument of mourning stand.

557 (x. lxii)

Spare, master, spare the innocents. So may
The long-haired rascals crowd your feast to-day;
Your class adore you; no arithmetician
Or short-hand fiend endanger your position.
The Lion's breath now burns the cloudless days,
The harvest swelters in the noon-tide blaze;

Put by the cat of savage Scythian hide,
Foul courtier of your throne, with murder dyed
Of Phrygian Marsyas. Put by the cane,
That brutal symbol of your tyrant reign.
Till mid October hide the cruel stuff;
In summer, if they're well, boys learn enough.

558 (x. lxv)

You call yourself Corinthian, none denies,
Charmenion, but to my great surprise
You hail me "brother," me of Tagus strain,
Thoroughbred chestnut out of Celt by Spain.
Are we so like? Your hair is kempt and curly,
Mine is of Spanish broom and stiff and surly.
You're smooth with dainty plaister, but my chest
And legs are hairy. With a lisp you speak;
Louder my reed can squeak. Less like appear
Eagle and dove, fierce lion and timid deer.
Wherefore forbear to call me "brother," pray,
Or I shall call you "sister," some fine day.

559 (x. lxvi)

What reckless tyranny, what savage taste
Could Theopompus on a kitchen waste?
Dare any man with soot besmirch that face
And those fair locks with grease and fire disgrace?
Who rather with a cup and glass should stand
And mix Falernian wine with cunning hand.
If such a doom such heavenly form awaits,
Jove's Ganymede may change his cups for plates.

560 (x. lxix)

You have the husband's latch-key, he has none;
You are the grey mare, Polla, when all's done.

561 (x. lxx)

If scarce one book I issue in a year,
Learned Politus, idle I appear.
That I should publish one should more surprise;
Think only how my scanty leisure flies.
Grey morning spent in visits unreturned;
Congratulations paid and never earned;
My seal to set at fair Lucina's shrine*;
Nor seven o'clock nor noon is ever mine.
Consul or praetor or some temple throng
Detain me; poets chatter all day long.
Who dare refuse when advocates invite,
Or rhetorician or grammarian slight?
After the bath at four I seek the dole
Tired out. And who will fill my little scroll?

* A business resort.

562 (x. lxxi)

You who would wish your sire a green old age,
Cherish this stone and read the sculptured page.
The good Rabirius' parents here repose;
Old age was ne'er so blissful at the close.
At sixty years they met a gentle end
Of life and wedlock; to one pyre they wend.
He grieves as for a thread untimely rent;
'Tis sheer perversity, this sad lament.

563 (x. lxxii)

ON THE ACCESSION OF NERVA

In vain you stand, soft Flattery, at my gate
And in smooth accents mourn your hapless fate.
No "lord and master" claims my service due;
There's no more occupation here for you.
Away! The turban'd Parthian's praise repeat
And kiss the dust beneath a monarch's feet.
There is no despot here, but counsellor
In peace supreme, lord paramount in war.
With maiden tresses bare and rustic weeds
From Stygian prison-house lost Truth he leads.
Under such presidency, Rome, reflect
And get thyself another dialect.

564 (x. lxxiii)

Kind gift, friend eloquent, your letter brings,
Of rich Italian stuff, a robe for kings.
Austere Fabricius, should he rise, would scorn it,
Maecenas or Apicius might have worn it.
A two-fold value on the giver turns;
Not every sacrifice a blessing earns.
Enough; 'tis yours; and were the rest no claim,
I'ld hail it, Marcus, for our common name.
But more than either gift or name the voice
Of friendship charms me and a critic's choice.

565 (x. lxxiv)

Cease, cruel Rome, to do your client wrong!
The courtier wearies of his task. How long

Shall friends be docketed with grooms and pages
At fifty halfpence for a day's whole wages,
When Scorpus* for one brief victorious thrill
His fifty money-bags with gold can fill?
Not for Apulian pasture lands I sue,
My verse to recompense, if aught be due;
Hybla delights not me nor fruitful Nile
Nor dainty bloom of Setia's grapes that smile
Upon the Pomptine marshes from the steep;
What, then, is my petition? Let me sleep.

* A jockey.

566 (x. lxxvi)

Fortune, does this seem fair? Here is a man,
No knight from Cappadocian caravan,
Parthian or Scythian, but true breed of Rome
In tent of Remus reared or Numa's home,
Good man, good comrade and good scholar he,
But has one fault, a great one, poetry.
Maevius in fustian shivers, while the varlet
Who rides for Caesar goes ablaze in scarlet.

567 (x. lxxvii)

PROFESSIONAL ETIQUETTE

Carus in dying played a shabby game;
    That fever, Maximus, was far too rough.
    An ague would have been severe enough;
There was no hurry till the doctor came.

568 (x. lxxviii)

Macer, to fair Salonae's coast you'll flee.
Take with you honour, justice, purity.
So office comes home poorer. Golden strand,
Send back your ruler with an empty hand,
Wish him to linger, and, when he departs,
Attend him with regret but grateful hearts.
I, Macer, in the savage land of Spain
Shall ever think of you with longing pain.
No page of mine with reed of Tagus penned
But shall to Macer's name its witness lend.
So with the chosen few may I be reckoned,
By you a classic to Catullus second.

569 (x. lxxix)

Torquatus has a house four miles from Rome;
There Otacilius bought a humble home.
One built a bath of mottled marbles new,
His rival made a wash-house copper do.
Torquatus planted bay-trees in a row,
The fool must needs a hundred chestnuts sow.
Torquatus consul, he was village mayor,
Thinking his job a very big affair.
Torquatus, like the ox whose bulk rehearsed
Killed the poor frog, will Otacilius burst.

570 (x. lxxx)

Eros laments when dappled agate ware
Or costly slave he spies or citron rare,
And sighs again to think that if he could
He'ld buy the whole contraption as it stood.

How many, Eros, are like you inside,
And smile discreetly at the tears they hide.

571 (x. lxxxii)

If my discomfort pander to your ease,
I'll dress and call at midnight, if you please,
Dare the fierce blast of the inclement north,
And, rain and snow unheeding, sally forth.
But you'll not have one penny more to show
For torturing a freeborn Roman so.
Gallus, forbear, my useless labour end,
Which helps not you but punishes your friend

572 (x. lxxxiii)

TO ONE WHO HIDES HIS BALDNESS

Your scattered side-locks to a bunch you train,
And draw a forest to the shining plain.
Then comes the wind, and once again are seen
Two curly masses with a space between.
Spendophorus and Telesphorus you'ld swear
And Hermerotes in the midst were there.
Be one, Marinus; your old age confess;
A bald coot feathered vaunts his ugliness.

573 (x. lxxxv)

That old salt Ladon, who the wherry plied,
Built him a house close by his native tide.
There raging Tiber, swollen by winter rain,
Flooding the neighbour land came down amain.

Drawn up above the waters' utmost marge
He lined with stones his weather-beaten barge
And stemmed the flow. Oh strange! The sunken bark
To its mechanic master proved an ark.

574 (x. lxxxvi)

Laurus was deep in love. With what? A ball.
No other heart such passion did enthral.
To lesser players once he gave the law:
Himself a plaything* now, a man of straw.

* A stuffed figure used in games: the "dummy" of Ep. 87.

575 (x. lxxxvii)

October's Kalends! Pious Rome, I pray,
Remember Restitutus' natal day.
Be kind with voice and prayer. Peace, law-courts, peace!
Let the poor client's waxen taper cease,
Mean tablets, paltry napkins*, let them freeze
Until December's gay festivities.
Let richer folk with costly offerings vie,
The purse-proud merchant send his native dye;
Let culprits caught for drunken brawling late
Send purple vestments to their advocate;
Let the chaste matron rescued from a fix
With her own hand send genuine sardonyx;
Let ancient connoisseurs their gifts impart
Of precious plate engraved by Phidias' art.
Let farmers send a kid, sportsmen a hare,
Anglers their quarry from the river bear.
If each man sends his own, what do you think
Shall be the poet's present? Pen and ink.

* Presents from poor clients. Compare Ep. 186.

576 (x. lxxxviii)

TO AN IDLER

Cotta, each praetor's notice still you scan,
And read your letters too: you busy man.

577 (x. lxxxix)

ON A STATUE

Juno, the crown of Polyclitus' fame,
That even Phidias had deigned to claim,
On Ida's top that day*, she shines so fair,
Would without doubt have triumphed o'er the pair.
Were Jove to Juno not a lover true,
He would adore the Juno carved by you.

* Referring to the judgment of Paris.

578 (x. xcii)

Marius, like me, true friend of tranquil rest,
Of old Atina's citizens noblest, best,
Guard well my twins, the glory of the wold,
My own dear pines, and oaks by Faun patrolled,
And my untutored farm-wife's altars two,
One for Silvanus, and one, Jove, for you,
Bedewed by kid and goat, and Dian's shrine,
Fair hallowed precinct of the maid divine,
And dainty Flora's bay-encircled glade
Where she her refuge from Priapus made.
Whene'er with blood or incense you entreat
Some guardian power of this my modest seat,
Say, thy own Martial, wheresoe'er he be,
Offers this willing sacrifice to thee,
An absent priest; pray think him present here
And grant to both the friends what each holds dear

579 (x. xciii)

If, Clemens, to Patavium first you go
And see the slopes with mantling vines aglow,
These lines ere published to Sabina bear,
Now newly clad in purple mantle fair.
A rose fresh plucked delights while still unspoiled,
So poems by no vulgar greeting soiled.

580 (x. xciv)

WITH A PRESENT OF BOUGHT APPLES

No Libyan serpent guards my apple-tree,
Alcinous' orchard pays no toll to me:
Nomentum-grown, my trees in safety live,
And thieves to waxy fruit a wide berth give.
These then I send you of Suburra's brand,
A tribute of my labour, not my land.

581 (x. xcvi)

Strange that I write of nations far away,
Avitus, though in Latium grown grey,
Thirst for the golden Tagus, and would fain
'Mid Salo's humble plenty live again.
That land is dear, in which a small estate
Enriches me and simple wealth seems great.
We feed the land, they by the land are fed;
Our hearth is scant and dim, theirs glowing red.
Here famine's dear, and ruin mocks the board;
There the kind earth supplies the larder's hoard.
One summer here spoils togas four or more,
There one coat does for me for autumns four.
Go, cringe to friends, Avitus, court the great,
That soil will give you treasure while you wait.

582 (x. xcvii)
>The funeral pile upreared, papyrus laid,
>The corpse with perfumes and with tears arrayed,
>Grave, bier, attendants, all as it should be,
>Numa revived. He had left all to me.

583 (x. xcix)
>If Socrates had Roman ancestry,
>Rufus among the Satyrs* he would be.
>
>* Ugly but better than he looks.

584 (x. c)
>Why, blockhead, mix your verse with mine, and claim
>That ill-joined whole, when half puts half to shame?
>Why seek to pair the fox and lion? Why
>Bid mousing owls abreast of eagles fly?
>Had you a leg from Ladas*, little good
>Were one fleet limb, if t'other were of wood.
>
>* A famous race-horse.

585 (x. ci)
>If Gabba, ancient wit, returned once more,
>Caesar's pet jester, from the Elysian shore,
>Who saw Capitolinus take him down,
>"Peace, Gabba," he would say; "you're just a clown."

586 (x. ciii)
>Townsmen, on lofty Bilbilis who shiver,
>Bred on the bank of Salo's rushing river,
>Pray are you glad to know your poet's fame?
>He is the pride and glory of your name.
>At poor Verona is Catullus known,
>Fain would she claim my verses as her own.

Now four and thirty summers Rome has passed
Since I partook your harvest revels last;
And, while within the imperial walls I stay,
The Italian sky has seen my locks turn grey.
Welcome the prodigal, I'll come to Spain;
If you're unfriendly, I'll to Rome again

587 (x. civ)

Go, little book, and with a favouring tide
To Flavus o'er the waste of waters glide.
With easy course and wafting breezes go
And seek the heights of Spanish Tarraco.
High Bilbilis you'll see and Salo far
After five changes of your hurrying car.
What is my message? My few friends you'll see,
For four and thirty winters lost to me.
Greet them at once and bid my Flavus keep
A pleasant corner for me, one that's cheap,
To give your master tranquil ease. That's all;
I hear the peremptory captain call.
He chides delay. I see your canvas swell
Before the breeze. My little book, farewell!

588 (xi. i)

Well, little book, and whither off so gay
In Tyrian mantle pranked for holiday?
To see Parthenius*? You'll return unread.
He reads, not books, but humble prayers instead.
If he had time for poetry, he'ld find
Time for his own. You think that fortune's kind,

* Ep. 217.

If to some humble reader's hand you go.
Then seek Quirinus' neighbouring portico.
Pompey, Europa, Jason*, no such throng
Can boast that sits and loiters all day long.
Among them two or three will fumble o'er
My simple nonsense, food for moths before,
When betting gossip and the latest tale
Of Scorpus or of Incitatus† fail.

* Fashionable resorts.   † A horse.

589 (XI. ii)

Hence, puritanic scowl and churlish frown
And rigid morals of a country clown;
The daylight shall not save you! Get you hence,
Affected prudery and nice pretence!
My verse "A merry Christmas" cries to all,
With such a prince a fair and welcome call.
Let crusty readers hail rough Santra's line.
We will not think of them; this book is mine.

590 (XI. iii)

Not idle city crowds alone I please,
Nor are the ears that hear me all at ease.
The stiff centurion thumbs me in the snow,
To foughten fields in Getic frost I go.
The Briton's said to quote me. After all
What's fame? No fortune answers to my call.
What everlasting poems could I write,
What battle-fields with trumpet blast indite,
If Fate Augustus would to earth restore
And bountiful Maecenas as of yore!

591 (XI. iv)

TO NERVA

Gods, who from Troy Aeneas would that day
Before his burning treasure bear away,
Immortal Jove, now first in gold arrayed,
His consort, and that blue-eyed motherless maid*,
With Janus, who first crowned our Nerva's head,
Thrice consul, smile upon my hands outspread.
Preserve our chief, preserve our senate too;
May they reflect his virtues, he renew.

* Athene, the Roman Minerva.

592 (XI. v)

The same.

Caesar, what's right and fair is dear to you.
So Numa felt, but then he'd not a sou.
Riches sap morals; hard it is to find
A ten-fold Croesus with a Numa's mind.
Could we our sires of mighty name recall
And leave untenanted Elysium's hall,
Camillus freedom's champion would adore,
Fabricius from your hand take golden ore.
Brutus would serve you gladly, Sulla dread
Forgo his crown to place it on your head.
Caesar and Pompey both should love you well,
For you rich Crassus in a cottage dwell.
Could Cato's self return from Pluto's tide
To visit earth, he'ld be on Caesar's side.

593 (XI. vi)

Hail, jolly Christmas, time of liberty,
Now may our slaves be like their masters free.

You laugh, 'tis not forbidden. Hence, wan care,
What's uppermost without restraint we'll dare.
Fill me such goblets as in days of yore
Pythagoras to tyrant Nero bore;
Fill, Dindymus, no shirking; water's stuff;
Let me drink deep, I shall have themes enough.
Come, kiss me. If you count Catullus-wise*,
You'll have Catullus' sparrow † for your prize.

* An impossible number imagined by Catullus.
† The pet of Catullus' Lesbia.

594 (XI. viii)

Sweet as the balsam drop from eastern trees
Or withered saffron ravished by the breeze,
As apples in the winter mellowing
Or luscious first-fruits of the lusty spring,
Like silken raiment from an empress' chest
Or amber by a maid's warm finger pressed,
Falernian old from distant bin exuding
Or bees above Sicilian garden brooding,
Or perfumed vase or holy maiden's vow,
Or wreath fresh fallen from a rich man's brow—
Why swell the list? Take all this galaxy,
So sweet my page-boy's morning kiss to me.

595 (XI. ix)

Crowned with Jove's oak-leaves, glory of our stage,
Here Memor's portrait breathes from age to age.

596 (XI. x)

Turnus writes satire, bending from the height
Of tragedy, lest he his brother slight.

598 (XI. xii)
Doles you may beg for children seven or eight:
For parents, Zoilus, you'll have to wait*.
* Compare for the dole Ep. 501, for Zoilus 529.

599 (XI. xiii)
Who tread the wide Flaminian way
Pass not this noble tomb, I pray.
The town's delight, the wit of Nile,
A kindly art, a merry smile,
Our honour and our grief lie here
Accompanying poor Paris' bier.
No love or Cupid can be found;
They lie with Paris underground.

600 (XI. xiv)
A DWARF'S EPITAPH
Burial, kind heirs, your tiny kinsman spare,
One grain of sand is more than he could bear.

601 (XI. xviii)
You gave me, friend, a snug retreat
As cosy as my window seat.
A garden? No! a woodland chaste
Within a cricket's leap embraced;
An ant with dinner it provides,
And in a folded kerchief hides.
Of grass about as much it grows
As it of spice and pepper knows.
A cucumber would burst its pale,
A serpent leave out half his tail.
A single crab could not grow fat
And forage fails the dying gnat.

My ploughman small the mole I call;
The mushroom has no room at all;
The way-side fig-tree does not cheer
Nor violet spread its petals here.
A mouse's rage the frontier gores
More fell than Calydonian boar's*.
My little crop would serve at best
To build a flying swallow's nest.
Priapus† bulks not half his size,
And harvest in a snail-shell lies.
A nut-shell is my vat and bin.
—What mischief lies in words akin!
You would have found it little harder
To save your land and share your larder.

    * Ep. 306, note.   † A boundary post representing a god.

602 (XI. xxiv)

When I escort you on your walk
Attentive to your idle talk,
And on each word and action smile,
What poems could be born the while!
Pray does not this seem loss to you?
Rome reads, the stranger loves me too.
Grave knights approve, great nobles prize,
Law puffs, and poets criticize.
You kill it all, I cannot bear it,
Greedy Labullus: hear me swear it.
Simply to swell your clients' roll
You of my poetry take toll.
A month scarce sees a single line,
That comes when bards go out to dine

603 (XI. xxxi)

Atreus served up a nephew—and a niece—meal;
Cruel Caecilius chops cucumber piecemeal.
First as a whet, three courses it pervades,
Now as a final savoury masquerades.
The baker kneads of it insipid cakes,
Or shapes and patterns in confection makes;
Dates dear to theatres and mincemeat rare,
You'ld think the lentil and the bean were there.
Haggis and mushrooms will he imitate
And tiny sprats and tail of tunny great.
The still-room man with cunning instinct true
Dresses and flavours it with leaves of rue.
So he fills up his dishes great and small
And oblong polished platters one and all.
High taste and style he reckons that to be,
A dozen dishes at a penny's fee.

604 (XI. xxxii)

TO ONE WHO AFFECTED EXTREME POVERTY

You have no toga, hearth or bug-trod bed,
A dripping thatch of reed protects your head.
You have no homebred servants young or old,
Nor dog nor cup nor bar nor key to hold.
Yet, destitute of all, you have the face
Among the decent poor to claim a place.
A phantom, Nestor, is the pride you nurse;
There's nothing decent in an empty purse.

605 (XI. xxxiii)

Greenjacket, proud of many a prize before,
After his patron's death won many more.
His fame's immortal, vainly you attack it;
Not Nero was the winner but Greenjacket.

606 (XI. xxxiv)

Aper has bought a mansion which no owl
Would call his own, it is so old and foul.
Maro's a fine house in the neighbourhood.
Aper, ill-lodged, will find his dinner good.

607 (XI. xxxv)

You ask a crowd, Fabullus, and complain
That I when you invite me still abstain.
You wonder, argue, threaten legal action;
For me to dine alone has no attraction.

608 (XI. xxxvi)

My Julius marks this day with stone of white.
My prayers are answered and he glads my sight.
His thread seemed broken and his end was near;
They feel less joy, who have had less to fear.
Hypnus, awake! Pour the immortal wine,
Such prayers when answered claim a cask divine;
Five measures full and six and eight again,
To Caius, Julius, Proculus I'll drain.

609 (XI. xxxvii)

THE RICH SLAVE AGAIN

Why, Zoilus, on your finger must you fix
Rich gold and gems and waste a sardonyx?
That ring but lately girt your ankle round,
But for a finger 'twill less fit be found.

* See Ep. 73, note.

610 (XI. xxxviii)

Bids for a teamster, Aulus, lately mounted
To twenty thousand: 'twas his deafness counted.

611 (XI. xxxix)

TO AN OLD SERVANT

You rocked my cradle, Charidemus dear,
You were my childhood's guardian ever near.
The napkin with my shaven beard grows black,
Pricked by my lips my lady cries "Alack!"
To you I have not grown; the bailiff fears you,
The steward's in awe; the household all reveres you.
I'm not allowed to gamble or to woo;
I'm to be nothing; all's permitted you.
You check, you watch, you draw deep sighs, complain,
Scarce from the birch your anger will refrain.
With perfumed locks I walk in rich attire;
You cry "For shame! Far otherwise your sire!"
With frowning brow you count each cup I drink;
The cellar that I draw from's yours, I think.
Peace, freedman, peace, in Cato's mantle drest;
There's one I know my manhood will attest.

612 (XI. xli)

Proud of his pigs, their fame and corporation,
Amyntas planned for them a rich collation.
He climbed an oak to shake the teeming mast,
The boughs gave way, the rider followed fast.
His father doomed the oak-tree to the pyre
To expiate the crime and feed the fire.
Lygdus, be warned then by your neighbour's fate
And tell your herd by tail and not by weight.

613 (XI. xlii)

You ask for lively epigrams, but send
Dull themes, Caecilianus. Well, my friend?
Hymettus' honey, Hybla's would you see?
Corsican thyme's no food for Attic bee.

614 (XI. xlviii)

Here Silius, master now where Cicero
Once lingered, Virgil's monument doth show.
None else, methinks, had orator or bard
Desired his ashes or his home to guard.

615 (XI. xlix)

A poor man's loyalty availed to save
Illustrious Virgil's half-forgotten grave.
Silius resolved his memory to uprear;
His rival genius made the gift more dear.

616 (XI. l)

Phyllis, from hour to hour, from day to day
You rob my folly. I'm your cunning's prey.
Your crafty handmaid weeps a mirror gone,
Gem from your finger, from your ear a stone.
A stolen silk dress you turn to gain, and ask
Me to refill with scent your empty flask.
Now for a jar of crusted wine you pray,
Some chattering witch will charm your dreams away,
Or I must bring you for some rich friend's feast
A two-pound mullet, or a pike at least.
To common fairness some regard is due;
Then treat me kindly, dear, as I treat you.

617 (XI. lii)

Julius*, I hope you'll dine with me at home.
If you've no better invitation, come.
After we've bathed—it's two, you understand,—
(Stephanus' bath, you know, is close at hand)
First lettuce, good digestion to bespeak,
And the green toppings of a wholesome leek,
Old whitebait bigger than an infant tunny
With eggs and rue in all due ceremony.
Yet other eggs, but dressed in gentle heat,
And cheese from smoke-jets of Velabrum sweet,
And olives mellowed by Picenum's cold;
This for a whet; the rest you'll now be told.
I lie to tempt you; "udder, oysters, fish,
Fat birds from coop and marsh to meet your wish:
Seldom on Stella's board such cates you view";
Nay, better still, I'll not recite to you.
* Cerealis.

Rather yourself your "Giants" may rehearse
And rustic themes in godlike Virgil's verse.

618 (XI. liii)

Claudia, though sprung of British rider blue,
Might be a wife of Roman lineage true.
How fair she is! She seems Italian born,
The Athenian capital she might adorn.
She owns a blessing on her faithful bed,
And hopes to see her sons and daughters wed.
Pray God her one dear husband still to spare
And glad her eyes with three men-children fair

619 (XI. liv)

Unguent and cassia from the funeral pyre,
And half-charred incense from its inmost fire,
And spice that from the bed of death you stole,
From that foul toga, Zoilus*, unroll.
Your feet have sent your wanton hands astray;
You're now a thief, who were a runaway.

* Ep. 73.

620 (XI. lv)

When Lupus swears he hopes you'll get a son,
There's nothing, Urbicus, he less wants done.
The skilful hunter hides his true intent;
He bids you do, what he would fain prevent.
Let but Cosconia hint a family
Then Lupus will be paler far than she.
Still, when you die, 'twere best beyond all question
That he should think you'd followed his suggestion.

621 (XI. lvi)

Stoic, you give to death too much laudation.
Your fortitude expects my admiration.
Why, 'tis but parting from your chipped tureen,
Chaeremon, and your fire that is not in,
Your truckle-bed, your mat for bugs to play in,
And shabby toga you spend night and day in.
Transcendent soul, who vinegar can lack
And bid farewell to straw and victual black!
But should you soft and downy cushions get
And fleecy purple rug for coverlet,
How you would long to reach thrice Nestor's span
And live each single moment that you can!
Life to despise is easy when you're poor:
Give me the man, who, starving, can endure.

622 (XI. lvii)

Am I too bold, Severus, poet mine,
To send you verse, who deign with me to dine?
Jove, though with nectar and ambrosia blest,
Is yet with wine and unbaked meats addressed.
His bounty's given you all; if what's your own
Be gift displeasing, then you've room for none.

623 (XI. lix)

By day and night Charinus wears
A load of rings; in all he airs
     Some thirty brace.
Even at the bath he keeps them going,
You ask the cause to which it's owing;
     He has no case.

624 (XI. lxv)

Some hundred guests are due by invitation
To join you in your birthday celebration.
I was not last of old your board to grace,
Justinus; no one grudged my honoured place.
Another day you serve the scraps again;
To-day the crowd; I'll keep your birthday then.

625 (XI. lxix)

Bred of the amphitheatre's hunting race,
A lamb at home, a lion in the chase,
My name was Lydia, Dexter's comrade true,
Whom he preferred, Erigone's hound, to you,
Or Cephalus' Cretan dog, who with him clomb
The skies and shares his master's starry home.
Me no unprofitable time's decay
Consumed, as Argus from his lord away,
But lightning tusk of such fell monster slew
As Calydon* or Erymanthus† knew.
Although too soon I yield my latest breath,
I could not perish by a nobler death.

* Ep. 326.   † Scene of the boar-hunt of Hercules.

626 (XI. lxxvi)

You press for my ten thousand, Paetus, sore
    For that two hundred thousand Bucco lost you;
Why should I smart for others? Say no more;
    My debt considerably less will cost you.

627 (XI. lxxix)

To the first stone I came at four o'clock;
For laziness you'ld have me in the dock.
Paetus, the fault's not mine, for 'twas your loan
Conveyed me; I've no mule-team of my own.

628 (XI. lxxx)

AN ANSWER TO AN INVITATION TO BAIAE

Blest home of Venus, Baiae's golden coast,
Of nature's kindly gifts the proudest boast.
Though I devote a thousand verses to it,
I cannot, I am certain, justice do it.
And yet to sacrifice myself I'm loth;
You cannot reasonably want us both;
And if kind fortune granted you the prayer,
We should not make a comfortable pair.

629 (XI. lxxxii)

Philostratus, a guest returning late
    From Sinuessa home at midnight deep,
Well-nigh succumbed to poor Elpenor's fate*
    By tumbling headlong from a landing steep.
Nymphs†, he had not so nearly broke his head,
If he had been your sober guest instead.

* See Homer, *Od.* XI. 57.   † The water nymphs of the Spa.

630 (XI. lxxxiii)

Your guests are wealthy bachelors;
Was ever paid such rent as yours?

631 (XI. lxxxiv)

Unless in haste to reach the Stygian harbour,
Shun, if you're wise, Antiochus the barber.
Less fierce the knife yon white-armed votary gashes,
Whom Cybele's pipe to wild delirium lashes.
More gently Alcon will a hernia clear
Or broken bone more delicately shear.
Let him shave Stoic chins and Cynics rude
Or horses of their dusty manes denude.
Should he serve poor Prometheus on his peak,
He'ld bare his breast and beg the vulture's beak.
The tell-tale scars you see upon my face,
Such as a veteran boxer's brow disgrace,
'Tis no wife's ten commandments' angry brand;
Antiochus betrays his blade and hand.
The clever he-goat is not treated thus;
He wears a beard; he fears Antiochus.

632 (XI. lxxxvi)

Parthenopaeus, you'd a hacking cough;
The doctors ordered for its taking off
Honey and nuts and cakes, unwholesome diet,
And lollipops that keep the class-room quiet.
And yet all day you're coughing more or less;
There's nothing wrong with you but greediness.

633 (XI. xci)

Here lies, poor child, Aeolian Canace.
Her seventh winter was her last to be.
"Foul murder!" Traveller, shed no hasty tear;
Life's shortness should awake no murmur here.

Worse was the shape of death; a foul disgrace
Of eating cancer seized her dainty face.
Her very lips the fell disease did sear,
And grudged its lovely victim to the bier.
If she was destined to so brief a stay
Fate might have fallen in a kindlier way,
But death made haste to close her utterance fair;
Else she had moved stern Lachesis by her prayer.

634 (XI. xciii)

Where were ye, Muses, when in angry flame
Sank Pye's* Pierian dwelling? Phoebus, shame!
Oh cruel sin, oh scandal to the sky,
To bake the Pye-dish and forget the Pye!

* "Better to err with Pope than shine with Pye." Byron, *E.B.S.R.* 91.

635 (XI. xcvi)

This is kind Marcius' fount, not cradled Rhine:
Give place, rude German; 'tis the boy's, not thine.
Nor is it fitting that the victor wave
Deny its master for a captive slave.

637 (XI. cii)

It was no libel, Lydia, to declare
That not your face but cheeks alone were fair.
If silent, whether lying down or seated,
You'ld seem in wax or painting counterfeited.
But when you speak your cheeks are ugly too;
None so ill-treated by her voice as you.
Mind the authorities don't hear and see;
A talking statue bodes calamity.

638 (XI. cvii)

My book unrolled from title-page to end
Back, Septicianus, as read through, you send.
"Quite true, delighted, that's the style, hurray!"
I've often read five books of yours that way.

639 (XI. cviii)

A POSTSCRIPT

Contented reader—I had thought to say;
But something's wanting? Then perhaps you'll pay.
My bailiff's broke, my lads for victuals cry;
What? Silent? Can't afford it? Then good-bye.

640 (XII. iii)

My book, once wont to go abroad from Rome,
Now for the City leave my distant home,
Leave golden Tagus and rough Salo's strand,
A mighty nation and my native land.
Yet foreigner or stranger none may call you,
Rome's archives with your brethren shall instal you.
Of your own right you'll seek the new-built shrine,
And stately mansion of the Sisters Nine.
Or, if you'ld rather, by Suburra wend
And lordly mansion of my consul friend.
There Stella, crowned of eloquence the king,
Drinks unreproved of Ianthean spring,
A true Castalia, proud and strong and clear,
'Tis said, its virtue could the Muses cheer.
To people, knights and senators he'll speed you
And haply with a moistened eyelid read you.
A title? Verses read but two or three,
All will cry out the poems come from me.

641 (XII. v)

Two books, the tenth and the eleventh in date,
Came short in matter through our labour's strait*.
Thou, Caesar†, givest us leisure: so shall some
Read more, thou only this; the rest may come.

    * Referring to the tyranny of Domitian.   † Nerva.

642 (XII. vi)

In Nerva's palace gentle counsels reign,
And poetry resumes her whole domain.
Faith, lawful rule and smiling clemency
Revive; our ancient terrors turn to flee.
This is the world's, the pious Roman's prayer,
May such another be your long-lived heir.
Heaven bless you: such rare heart, such honest name
Numa or Cato's genial half might claim.
Your bounty bids our humble fortunes grow;
The kindly gods would scarce enrich us so.
Now truth is lawful, but you dared to be
An honest man in times of tyranny.

643 (XII. ix)

Kind Caesar, Palma rules my native Spain;
A willing captive, she has peace again.
With thanks we recognize your gracious hand
And greet your virtues in our native land.

644 (XII. xi)

Muse, to Parthenius* kindly greeting bring,
For who drinks deeper of the Aonian spring?
Whose harp doth louder by Castalia swell?
Whom of his flock doth Phoebus love so well?

    * Ep. 217. He was still chamberlain under Trajan.

'Tis much to ask, can he the time afford,
Bid him commend this volume to our lord.
Four words alone the timid mite shall need
For introduction: "This your people read."

645 (XII. xiv)

Priscus, why tear away after the hare away
    On your fleet mare away out for a toss?
Faster and faster, you're courting disaster,
    You're quarry not master, the hare is the boss.

Snares in the level are, meadows the devil are,
    Though there's no dike, ditch or stone, they'll betray.
Many there'll be you know ready to push and go
    And join the raree-show. Steady, I pray.

Let those of meaner race, born in a humbler place,
    Hustle and go the pace. They won't be missed.
You're of true Roman stock, hewn from the native rock,
    Your death the world would shock. Priscus, desist!

If you must press your gee, tempting your destiny,
    Safer the risk will be, boars let us harry.
Why covet danger plain reckless of bridle rein?
    Oftener the huntsman's slain, friend, than the quarry

646 (XII. xv)

RELICS OF DOMITIAN

The treasures that adorned a palace late
To Roman eyes and gods are confiscate.
Gold blazes green with Scythian jewel faced,
And Jove acknowledges a Tarquin's taste.

These dainty cups the Thunderer's self might use,
Nor Ganymede to serve them would refuse.
Now, Jove, you're quite well off, and so are we,
But lately partners in adversity.

647 (XII. xvii)

The fever never leaves you, you complain,
Laetinus, it is there again, again.
It dines with you and bathes, and shares your store
At meals, of mushrooms, oysters, udder, boar.
With Setine and Falernian aglow
It cools its Caecuban with melted snow.
Nard stains its hair, its goblet roses crown,
And costly purples clothe its bed of down.
Your malady lies rich, and lives in clover,
You don't like that? Let Dama* take it over.

* A slave.

648 (XII. xviii)

HOME

While, Juvenal, perchance you restless stray
By Dian's hill or on our great highway,
Using your sweating toga as a fan,
Tramping the Caelian hill, unhappy man,
Long banished, I salute the rustic scene
And Bilbilis, of gold and iron queen.
Platea, Boterdus, harsh as sounded here,
My indolence with pleasant labour cheer.
Profound my slumber out of honest measure;
Scarce the third hour can wean me from its pleasure.
The time I squandered through a life-time past
Is now made good and credited at last.

A rough undress, (dress-suits are quite unknown)
When wanted, from some crazy chair is thrown.
I rise; a roaring fire of oak-wood glows
Home-gathered; round her pots the house-dame goes;
Now comes a huntsman such as sheltered brake
Ne'er saw, and, rustic plenty in his wake,
A dapper steward seeking heads to shear*.
There's joy in life and death has comfort here!

* Only personal slaves of the rich wore long hair. Now that is over.

649 (XII. xxi)

TO HIS SPANISH WIFE
See 656 below.

Marcella, born by bracing Salo's water,
Who would suppose you of my land a daughter?
So wise you are, so sweet. A single tone
Once heard would mark you for our princes' own.
Sure never blossom of such dainty hue
On Capitol or mid-Suburra grew,
Nor oft of foreign cradle flower so sweet
Again a Roman matron's name will greet.
You make me less regret my eastern home
In banishment, for you to me are Rome.

650 (XII. xxiii)

Your teeth and hair are borrowed, Laelia; fie!
Gold cannot purchase you another eye.

651 (XII. xxiv)

Dear quiet carriage, more delightful far
Than warlike chariot or two-horse car,
Accomplished Aelian's gift! Juvatus, here
You may repose your secrets in my ear.

No dusky acrobat on Libyan steed
Or high-girt courier will my car precede.
Mule-driver, pony-driver's far away.
Oh! were Avitus at my side to-day!
I should not fear a babbling tell-tale by.
How happily the livelong day would fly!

652 (XII. xxv)

I ask you for some money unsecured;
You've none, unless on mortgage 'tis assured.
What, Telesinus, you can't spare a friend
To faithless fruit and cabbages you lend.
You're charged with treason; say, will earth reply?
Condemned to exile; will a farm stand by?

653 (XII. xxvi)

You, master senator, your social round
Pursuing, rate me as a lazy hound,
Who will not range at dawn the streets of Rome
And, rich in kisses, limp exhausted home.
Your purpose is a title proud to gain
Or over Moor and Cappadocian reign.
But who am I, to rise before the lark
And brave the muddy terrors of the dark?
What is the end? My toe outstrips my shoe,
Down comes the deluge. "Mantle, where are you?"
I cry aloud, but there is none to hear.
A footman whispers in my tingling ear,
"Laetorius sends a hearty invitation."
Not at the price, man; I prefer starvation.
A province is your prize, but mine a pittance.
Equal desert demands an equal quittance.

654 (XII. xxviii)

An answer to Ep. 211.

I mix with water, Cinna, you refuse it;
There's nothing in the wine, it's how you use it.

655 (XII. xxix)

What Massa was to coinage, such or near
Such thief Hermogenes of woven gear.
Watch his right hand and grip his left hand tightly;
He'll filch your napkin, Pontius, more lightly
Than a stag's breath sucks in the clammy snake,
Or heavenly bow new moisture from the lake.
When wounded Myrinus claimed discharge that day,
Four handkerchiefs the rascal stole away.
The praetor his white kerchief would have thrown,
The wily scoundrel marked it for his own.
One day, when napkins were not safe to bring,
He from the table stole the covering.
This failing him, the very couch he'ld strip,
And from the table's foot the bandage rip.
Although the Circus swelters in the heat
The awning's drawn his wary steps to greet.
The flustered tars, when at the port he calls,
Furl close their canvas and look out for squalls.
The bald and surpliced priest of Isis flies
If 'mid her worshippers the rogue he spies.
To dinner never did he napkin bear,
But home returning still had one to spare.

656 (XII. xxxi)

These woods, these founts, this woven upland vine,
These winding, plashing runnels, all are mine;

These meads that rival Paestum's twice-blown rose,
And winter green not wanned by winter's snows,
The slimy eel that my own fishpond pens,
The dovecote white with snowy denizens,
Marcella's bounty*. Wanderer long and late,
This home she gave me and this modest state.
Were to my eyes Alcinous' garden shown
I'ld say, "Nausicaa, I prefer mine own."
* See Ep. 649 above.

657 (XII. xxxii)

Vacerra, shame of tenant tribe, I've seen
Your wife, with seven red elf-locks far between,
Your sister and your aged mother, bent
With chattels seizable for two years' rent;
'Twas like some gang of Furies gone astray.
Staring and wild you followed on your way;
Paler than ancient box your path you take,
A modern Irus trudging in their wake.
You'ld think all beggardom on travel sped
With two-legged board and three-legged truckle-bed.
A lantern and a cornel bowl were there,
And leaking crock of nameless household ware,
A rusty brazier and a crazy jar;
Foul garlic, sprats were wafted from afar.
'Twas like some stinking fishpond; add to these
Cheap penny-royal and Tolosan cheese,
Garlic and onion ropes with vacant spaces
And resin, cure for demi-damsels' faces.
Why seek a mansion, jeer at villadom?
The bridge* might be your cheap and nasty home.
* Typical haunt of beggars.

658 (XII. xxxiv)

WE TWA

> Three years, dear Julius, we've lived together,
> We've had some foul, but we've had more fair weather.
> Cast up a reckoning in black and white,
> The happier colour turns the balance quite.
> Would you a life without its bitters spend?
> Don't make of any man too close a friend.

659 (XII. xxxvi)

> Four pounds, or two, of silver to a friend
> Or freezing coat or scanty cloak you send;
> Or clinking coins that rattle in your hand,
> Which two or three months' wear and tear might stand.
> 'Tis all your gift, Labullus. You are kind?
> You're only good among the bad, you'll find.
> Give me the worthies of the days long past,
> Upon the honoured list you'll figure last.
> Tigris* outrun or Passerinus* fleet
> If you have speed. Let ass with ass compete.

* Race-horses.

660 (XII. xlv)

> Seeing your noddle bare
> Guarded with jealous care
> In kid-skin from the weather,
> It was a wag who said,
> Yours is the sweetest head
> That ever went in leather.

661 (XII. xlvi)

The public Gallus and Lupercus buys.
Now, Classicus, say poets are not wise.

662 (XII. xlvii)

O sweet and bitter in a breath,
    O genial comrade, crusty friend,
    Without thee life had instant end,
With thee to dwell were sudden death.

663 (XII. xlviii)

If boar and mushroom are plain fare to you,
And you don't think I value them, I do.
But they're not happiness; if I must pay
For five fat oysters in my will,—good-day!
Well, 'tis a grand repast, but for how long?
To-morrow, nay to-night, not worth a song.
From mullet, udder, hare, there's no way out
But sallow cheeks and agonizing gout.
No, not for princely feast your price I'ld pay
Or for the joys of pontiff's festal day.
Would heaven its nectar share and boast the favour,
Like treacherous Vatican* 'twould mar its flavour.
Seek other folk your humble guests to be,
Willing to bear your table's tyranny.
A friend would have me his pot-luck to share.
I'll dine with him; I can return such fare.

* A bad wine.

664 (XII. l)

You've bay and plane and soaring fir-trees old
And twenty swimming baths both hot and cold.
Your cloister's flanked by fifty pillars ample
And mottled marble for your feet to trample.
The fleet hoofs clatter in your riding-school,
To right and left are plashing fountains cool,
Halls long and wide; no room to dine or sleep in.
Why, what a gallant house no home to keep in!

665 (XII. li)

It is strange our Fabullinus
    Often duped has been?
No, the righteous like the bay-tree
    Flourish ever green.

666 (XII. lii)

Wont to enwreath his hair with Phoebus' bays
Nor less to plead and win the prisoner's praise,
Here lies, Sempronia, your Rufus true
Whose very ashes seem to sigh for you.
Your love will echo through the Elysian vale;
Even Helen's self will wonder at the tale.
Well done! False lover you forsook for true;
She, sought again, true love would not renew.
Atrides cherishes his wrongs no more;
Paris is guiltless; you have paid his score.
One day the Elysian fields will be your home;
No nobler shade to the bleak realms may come.
The Queen, herself a ravished maid's defence,
Will be still kinder to your penitence.

667 (XII. liii)

Paternus, though you're rich beyond compare,
You sit upon your pile and nothing share,
Like the great serpent, who, 'twas sung of old,
Kept watch upon the Scythian fleece of gold.
But there's a reason; this your vaunted plea,
You have a son of dread rapacity.
Try someone simpler to impose upon;
A miser father makes a spendthrift son.

668 (XII. lvi)

Every month, my Polycharmus,
With some ailment you alarm us,
Whose event is sure to harm us
    Though yourself no ill befall.
For each monthly convalescing
In return for such a blessing
Brings you gifts, our joy expressing.
    Can't you sicken once for all?

669 (XII. lvii)

Why to Nomentum do I oft repair,
My modest farm of stately comforts bare?
At Rome a poor man cannot sleep, think, rest;
Schoolmaster, baker, day and night infest.
He hears the whitesmith hammer all day long
And coiners clank their idle cricket song.
Yonder the Spanish goldsmith scares the day
And with his glittering mallet pounds away.
Frantic Bellona's rout the discord swells,
The bandaged sailor of his shipwreck tells;

The Jew home-tutored begs of passers-by,
And purblind hawkers sulphur matches cry.
He can tell o'er the hours of banished sleep,
Who can of cymbal beats the reckoning keep,
When the moon's blasted by the Colchian* spell.
You, Sparsus, cannot realize it well,
In the soft mansion of Petilius bred
That from its eyry views the mountain's head.
Your Roman garden with its town-bred hands
Excels the vintage of Falernian lands.
Your riding-school is closed, your slumber's deep,
No talk can wake, no ray unbidden peep,
No passing throng disturbs your city home:
I to my farm must flee; no rest in Rome.

* Medea came from Colchis. A witch could cause eclipses.

670 (XII. lx)

Name-day of Mars, when first in rosy light
I saw the forehead of the sun-god bright,
If my green altars and my country home
Misseem thee, honoured erst in lofty Rome,
Forgive me, that to-day I am no slave
But claim this brief exemption from the grave.
On one's own birthday discontent to fear
Because the water's cold, the wine not clear,
With careful hand the Caecuban to strain,
And play the waiter in one's own domain,
Greet new arrivals like an anxious host
And trample marble colder than the frost,
What reasonable man, I say, would choose
Such service as a menial might refuse?

671 (XII. lxii)

TO SATURN WHOSE FEAST WAS OUR CHRISTMAS
Written in Spain.

Lord of the ancient heavens, beneath whose reign
There was but tranquil ease, no toil, no pain,
No scope or need for Jove's avenging brand,
Ere yet the miner had embowelled the land,
Come with a smile to Priscus' royal feast,
Saturn, of all his guests not welcome least.
In the sixth frost you speed him home again
From Numa's peaceful Rome to distant Spain.
What festive pageantry these halls afford,
With plenty like a Roman market stored!
What bounteous wealth his lavish hands bestow,
What golden fountains to thy honour glow!
That the high festival new grace may boast,
A thrifty man and father is the host.
Wouldst thou win high esteem in far-off Spain?
Bid such a festival come oft again.

672 (XII. lxiii)

Richer than steep Venafrum, Corduba,
As perfect as the jar of Istria,
Whose flocks would shame Galaesus, not with stain
Of blood or purple feigned, but native grain,
Pray tell your poet not to circulate
Another's verses save at market rate.
Were he a decent writer I could stand it,
I could retaliate upon the bandit.
A bachelor steals your wife, redress you lack;
A blind man blinds you, you can't pay him back.

A penniless footpad's pretty safe, you know it;
But nothing's safer than a scurvy poet.

673 (XII. lxvi)

A thousand pounds is what your cottage cost;
And you would sell it cheaper, though you lost.
Amoenus, thus the purchaser you'ld cheat,
The costly fittings puff the paltry seat;
Couches that gleam with precious tortoiseshell
While citron slabs of Libyan forest tell;
Dumb-waiters to put gold and silver plate on,
And pages whom 'twere privilege to wait on.
Cost-price you double and "dirt cheap" exclaim:
Throw in the furniture, I'ld say the same.

674 (XII. lxvii)

Hermes was born in middle May,
Mid August is Diana's day;
Upon a mid October morn
Virgil, the sacred bard, was born.
May you still keep the other two,
Who give the poet's birth its due.

675 (XII. lxix)

Paulus, like pictures or like cups, for show
You keep your ancient friends and use them so.

676 (XII. lxx)

When Aper bathed, one knock-kneed slave attending,
His clothes a one-eyed beldame's cushion mending,
A ruptured wretch was there with oil to dress
This censor stern of bath-room drunkenness.

"Shatter the goblets, spill the wine," he'ld cry
If any knight after his bath was dry.
When lo! a fortune from an uncle's come;
A sober man he ne'er betakes him home.
Fine followers and rich wine-cups do their worst;
Aper when poor had never felt athirst.

677 (XII. lxxii)

You bought a crazy cote and tenement small
Hard by the graveyard of the slaughtered Gaul.
You left your pleading, your true property,
The small but certain income of your fee.
Pearl-barley, corn and millet, fare you well;
A farm must pay for you, a brief could sell.

678 (XII. lxxiv)

Pending your cargo of Egyptian glass
Three goblets from the circus well may pass.
The rarer gift might of presumption savour;
The common sort has two things in its favour;
No precious moulding fascinates the thief,
No heat the brittle texture brings to grief;
Besides, no eye need follow as we drink,
No hand need tremble on disaster's brink.
Again, if you for drinking healths should take them,
No harm would happen if you came to break them.

679 (XII. lxxvi)

THE OLD GRIEVANCE

A peck for four pence and a jar for twenty;
The farmer's bankrupt in the midst of plenty.

680 (XII. lxxviii)

Bithynicus, I never spoke you ill.
"No?" Must I swear? I'ld rather pay the bill.

681 (XII. lxxxi)

Last Christmas, Umber, his own cup not full,
Sent me a cape (inverted cup) of wool.
This year far richer—to give less were cruel—
He sends a full-sized porringer—for gruel.

682 (XII. lxxxii)

In heated bath or cool, try how you please,
You never can escape Menogenes.
Right hand or left he'll catch the tepid ball,
To you the honour of his toil will fall.
Your dusty feather-bag with cover slack
Though bathed and sandalled he will fetch you back.
Your scanty locks by the cut comb outspread
He'll call the tresses of Achilles' head.
He'll carry wine-lees from the chimney ripe,
And from your brow the perspiration wipe.
He'll be all praise and wonder, till you cry,
Worn out with toil, "Dine with me by and by."

683 (XII. lxxxvii)

Twice Cotta lost his shoes, unhappy man;
His slave was careless, so the story ran,
His one apology for suite and groom.
Necessity but gave invention room.
Determined not again such fate to meet
He went out dining on his naked feet.

684 (XII. lxxxviii)

Tongilianus I can answer for
As critic: he is that, if nothing more.

685 (XII. lxxxix)

Wool-wraps, Charinus, round your head you tie;
Hair-ache, not ear-ache is your malady.

686 (XII. xc)

Aloud prayed Maro for an aged friend
With burning semi-tertian near his end.
If the poor man from death he could recall,
A grateful victim to great Jove should fall.
The doctors gave a good report, and now
He prays that he may not fulfil his vow.

687 (XII. xcii)

You often ask me, Priscus, how I'ld use
My fortune if I stood in rich men's shoes.
'Tis hard forecasting the effect of pelf;
What sort of lion would you make, yourself?

688 (XII. xciv)

I started Epic and you followed me;
I closed my shutters, fearing rivalry.
I made the skirt a shift, strange transformation;
That instant, tragedy is your vocation.
I took to Lyric verse in Horace' vein;
Your monkey tactics bested me again.
I venture satire and you do the same;
Light elegies, and still you share the game.

In epigram I seek a humbler prize;
There too a rival in my path you rise.
You can't want everything: a bargain strike,
And leave me something you yourself dislike.

689 (XII. xcviii)

Fair Baetis, crowned with olive, by whose wide
And shimmering stream the golden fleece is dyed,
To Bacchus dear and Pallas, from whose home
Old Neptune spreads a broad sea-way to Rome,
Good luck to your new ruler, may this year
To all your peoples like the last be dear.
He knows that Macer's mantle's hard to wear;
Who shrewdly weighs his burden, he can bear.

690 (XIII. i)

For fear the whitebait should their mantle lack,
Olives their cloak and food the cockroach black,
Waste, Muse, my wretched paper. Christmas time,
The festive season, claims a merry rhyme.
I gamble not with knucklebones or dice;
Upon my table falls nor ace nor sice.
My nuts are paper and a pen my stakes;
Nor loss nor gain to me the main chance makes.

691 (XIII. ii)

Were you a critic whose unerring flair
Possessed a weight that Atlas could not bear,
Though you might laugh the great Latinus down*,
Self-buffeted, I fear no other clown.

* A comedian.

The tooth one bites with who would wish to bite?
The flesh is best, if you've an appetite.
Don't waste your labour. Save those reprehensions
For strutting peacocks; I have no pretensions.
Yet would I count for something, did I find you
In candid humour with no sun to blind you.

692 (XIII. iii)

These recipes are taken from the cook.
Four sesterces they charge you for the book.
Four is too much, you say? Then take two off it,
And Tryphon need not grumble at his profit.
A seasonable present they will be
From a poor friend by one as poor as he.
The titles tell you what it's all about;
If any do not suit you, leave them out.

693 (XIV. i)

The knights and senators in smart array
With our great lord keep merry holiday;
The ponds are freezing and the slave may shake
The dice-box nor in fear of prison quake.
Great folk and small folk, each may suit his mind;
Both rich and poor may here their prizes find.
"'Tis stuff and nonsense; nay! 'tis worse in sooth."
Quite so. Who would gainsay the naked truth?
Are Thebes, Troy, vile Mycenae to your taste?
"Go play with nuts." Nuts are too good to waste.
You may my limits at your choice define;
The stops are placed at every other line.

694 (Lib. Sp. i)

THE COLOSSEUM

> Egypt, your pyramids extol no more;
> Let not Assyria boast her wondrous store,
> Nor weak Ionians Trivia's ancient shrine
> Or Delos rich with offerings divine;
> You vaunting Carians, account not rare
> Your Mausoleum poised in empty air.
> To Caesar's Circus all must homage own:
> For many marvels now there's one alone.

695 (Lib. Sp. ii)

The same.

> Here, where Colossus climbs the starry seat,
> And proud abutments part the crowded street,
> A savage despot's halls extended wide;
> There was one house in Rome and none beside.
> Here, where the stately Circus meets our gaze
> High-towering, was a pond in Nero's days.
> Here, where the quick-built booth attracts the eye,
> A proud estate evicted poverty.
> Here, where the Claudian cloister spreads its gloom,
> A palace dwindled to its outmost room.
> Rome's night is ended. In the tyrant's seat
> For pastime, Caesar, bid thy people meet.

696 (Lib. Sp. iii)

> What race so savage and so far away
> But shares the pageant of thy Rome to-day?
> Here swain of Rhodope, to Orpheus rude,
> Sarmatian boor, whose team is drink and food;

Who secret Nile's remotest fountains drink
Or hear the breakers on the Ocean brink.
Each Arab, each Sabaean comes this way,
Cilicians wet with their own saffron spray;
The fierce Sigambrian with braided hair,
Aethiops with knotted tresses, hither fare,
With voices manifold but one accord
To hail their country's father and its lord.

697 (Lib. Sp. ix)

ON A RHINOCEROS

The Nose-horn, Caesar, that for recreation
You gave, in battle passed all expectation.
Well might the torrent of his wrath appal;
Bull found his master, and became a ball.

698 (Lib. Sp. xx)

Some for "Triumphus," some "Myrinus" cried;
Caesar, indulgent, neither boon denied.
Even thus he might have stilled a strife in jest;
So dear is pity to our hero's breast.

699 (Lib. Sp. xxii)

The same as 697.

Long time in gathering rage the monster bore
Each saucy thrust of trembling picador;
All hope of desperate conflict was in vain;
At length the wonted fury blazed again.
On his twin horns a bear he tosses clear
As play-ball gored by Andalusian steer.

700 (Lib. Sp. xxviii)

To give a sea-fight was Augustus' care
And rouse the waters with a trumpet's blare.
Far greater marvels grace our monarch's reign.
Nymphs see strange monsters rumbling in the main.
Triton beheld the foam-flecked chariots glow
And seemed again his master's team to know.
Nereus the fierce sea-conflict did array
Yet loth himself to tread the watery way.
Caesar, such pageant as thy fertile wave
Ne'er Amphitheatre or Circus gave.
Prate not of Nero's pool or Fucinus.
A true sea-battle was reserved for us.

701 (Lib. Sp. xxix)

Priscus and Verus fought in equal strife;
Long time in level balance hung their life;
For their dismissal many a shout was made;
But the just monarch his own law obeyed.
Still must they fight and lay the shield aside;
Viands and gifts he gave them, nought beside.
At last the struggle found an issue fair,
And equal victory and defeat they share.
To both were freedom and the palm assigned;
Such recompense did skill and valour find.
Who, Caesar, else but thee the law laid down
That two could merit, two receive the crown?

THE END

For EU product safety concerns, contact us at Calle de José Abascal, 56–1°,
28003 Madrid, Spain or eugpsr@cambridge.org.

www.ingramcontent.com/pod-product-compliance
Ingram Content Group UK Ltd.
Pitfield, Milton Keynes, MK11 3LW, UK
UKHW040616240426
470322UK00010B/145